Register Your Book

at ibmpressbooks.com/ibmregister

Upon registration, we will send you electronic sample chapters from two of our popular IBM Press books. In addition, you will be automatically entered into a monthly drawing for a free IBM Press book.

Registration also entitles you to:

- Notices and reminders about author appearances, conferences, and online chats with special guests

- Access to supplemental material that may be available

- Advance notice of forthcoming editions

- Related book recommendations

- Information about special contests and promotions throughout the year

- Chapter excerpts and supplements of forthcoming books

Contact us

If you are interested in writing a book or reviewing manuscripts prior to publication, please write to us at:

Editorial Director, IBM Press
c/o Pearson Education
800 East 96th Street
Indianapolis, IN 46240

e-mail: IBMPress@pearsoned.com

Visit us on the Web: ibmpressbooks.com

Implementing IBM®
Rational® ClearQuest®

IBM Press

The developerWorks® Series

T he IBM Press developerWorks Series represents a unique undertaking in which print books and the Web are mutually supportive. The publications in this series are complemented by their association with resources available at the developerWorks Web site on ibm.com. These resources include articles, tutorials, forums, software, and much more.

Through the use of icons, readers will be able to immediately identify a resource on developerWorks which relates to that point of the text. A summary of links appears at the end of each chapter. Additionally, you will be able to access an electronic guide of the developerWorks links and resources through ibm.com/developerworks/dwbooks that reference developerWorks Series publications, deepening the reader's experiences.

A developerWorks book offers readers the ability to quickly extend their information base beyond the book by using the deep resources of developerWorks and at the same time enables developerWorks readers to deepen their technical knowledge and skills.

For a full listing of developerWorks Series publications, please visit: **ibmpressbooks.com/dwseries**.

IBM Press

WEBSPHERE® BOOKS

IBM® WebSphere®
Barcia, Hines, Alcott, and Botzum

IBM® WebSphere® Application Server for Distributed Platforms and z/OS®
Black, Everett, Draeger, Miller, Iyer, McGuinnes, Patel, Herescu, Gissel, Betancourt, Casile, Tang, and Beaubien

Enterprise Java™ Programming with IBM® WebSphere®, Second Edition
Brown, Craig, Hester, Pitt, Stinehour, Weitzel, Amsden, Jakab, and Berg

IBM® WebSphere® and Lotus
Lamb, Laskey, and Indurkhya

IBM® WebSphere® System Administration
Williamson, Chan, Cundiff, Lauzon, and Mitchell

Enterprise Messaging Using JMS and IBM® WebSphere®
Yusuf

ON DEMAND COMPUTING BOOKS

Business Intelligence for the Enterprise
Biere

On Demand Computing
Fellenstein

Grid Computing
Joseph and Fellenstein

Autonomic Computing
Murch

RATIONAL® SOFTWARE BOOKS

Software Configuration Management Strategies and IBM Rational ClearCase®, Second Edition
Bellagio and Milligan

MORE BOOKS FROM IBM PRESS

Irresistible! Markets, Models, and Meta-Value in Consumer Electronics
Bailey and Wenzek

Service-Oriented Architecture Compass
Bieberstein, Bose, Fiammante, Jones, and Shah

Developing Quality Technical Information, Second Edition
Hargis, Carey, Hernandez, Hughes, Longo, Rouiller, and Wilde

Performance Tuning for Linux® Servers
Johnson, Huizenga, and Pulavarty

RFID Sourcebook
Lahiri

Building Applications with the Linux Standard Base
Linux Standard Base Team

An Introduction to IMS™
Meltz, Long, Harrington, Hain, and Nicholls

Search Engine Marketing, Inc.
Moran and Hunt

Inescapable Data
Stakutis and Webster

DB2® BOOKS

DB2® Universal Database V8 for Linux, UNIX, and Windows Database Administration Certification Guide, Fifth Edition
Baklarz and Wong

Understanding DB2®
Chong, Liu, Qi, and Snow

Integrated Solutions with DB2®
Cutlip and Medicke

High Availability Guide for DB2®
Eaton and Cialini

DB2® Universal Database V8 Handbook for Windows, UNIX, and Linux
Gunning

DB2® SQL PL, Second Edition
Janmohamed, Liu, Bradstock, Chong, Gao, McArthur, and Yip

DB2® Universal Database for OS/390 V7.1 Application Certification Guide
Lawson

DB2® for z/OS® Version 8 DBA Certification Guide
Lawson

DB2® Universal Database V8 Application Development Certification Guide, Second Edition
Martineau, Sanyal, Gashyna, and Kyprianou

DB2® Universal Database V8.1 Certification Exam 700 Study Guide
Sanders

DB2® Universal Database V8.1 Certification Exam 703 Study Guide
Sanders

DB2® Universal Database V8.1 Certification Exams 701 and 706 Study Guide
Sanders

DB2® Universal Database for OS/390
Sloan and Hernandez

The Official Introduction to DB2® for z/OS®, Second Edition
Sloan

Advanced DBA Certification Guide and Reference for DB2® Universal Database v8 for Linux, UNIX, and Windows
Snow and Phan

DB2® Express
Yip, Cheung, Gartner, Liu, and O'Connell

Apache Derby — Off to the Races
Zikopoulos, Baklarz, and Scott

DB2® Version 8
Zikopoulos, Baklarz, deRoos, and Melnyk

Implementing IBM® Rational® ClearQuest®

An End-to-End Deployment Guide

developerWorks® Series

Christian D. Buckley

Darren W. Pulsipher

Kendall Scott

IBM Press
Pearson plc
Upper Saddle River, NJ • Boston • Indianapolis • San Francisco
New York • Toronto • Montreal • London • Munich • Paris • Madrid
Capetown • Sydney • Tokyo • Singapore • Mexico City

Many of the designations used by manufacturers and sellers to distinguish their products are claimed as trademarks. Where those designations appear in this book, and the publisher was aware of a trademark claim, the designations have been printed with initial capital letters or in all capitals.

Copyright © 2007 International Business Machines Corporation. All rights reserved

The authors and publisher have taken care in the preparation of this book, but make no expressed or implied warranty of any kind and assume no responsibility for errors or omissions. No liability is assumed for incidental or consequential damages in connection with or arising out of the use of the information or programs contained herein.

Note to U.S. Government Users: Documentation related to restricted right. Use, duplication, or disclosure is subject to restrictions set forth in GSA ADP Schedule Contract with IBM Corporation.

IBM Press Program Managers: Tara Woodman, Ellice Uffer
Cover design: IBM Corporation

Published by Pearson plc
Publishing as IBM Press

IBM Press offers excellent discounts on this book when ordered in quantity for bulk purchases or special sales, which may include electronic versions and/or custom covers and content particular to your business, training goals, marketing focus, and branding interests. For more information, please contact:

> U.S. Corporate and Government Sales
> (800) 382-3419
> corpsales@pearsontechgroup.com

For sales outside the United States, please contact:

> International Sales
> international@pearsoned.com

The following terms are trademarks or registered trademarks of International Business Machines Corporation in the United States, other countries, or both: DB2, ClearQuest, CICS, IMS, Lotus, Tivoli, WebSphere, Rational, IBM, the IBM logo, and IBM Press. Java and all Java-based trademarks are trademarks of Sun Microsystems, Inc. in the United States, other countries, or both. Microsoft, Microsoft .Net, .NET, Windows, Windows NT, and the Windows logo are trademarks of the Microsoft Corporation in the United States, other countries, or both. Linux is a registered trademark of Linus Torvalds. Intel, Intel Inside (logo), MMX, and Pentium are trademarks of Intel Corporation in the United States, other countries, or both. OSF/1 and UNIX are registered trademarks, and The Open Group is a trademark of The Open Group in the United States and other countries. Eclipse is a trademark of Eclipse Foundation, Inc. Other company, product, or service names mentioned herein may be trademarks or service marks of their respective owners.

This Book Is Safari Enabled

The Safari® Enabled icon on the cover of your favorite technology book means the book is available through Safari Bookshelf. When you buy this book, you get free access to the online edition for 45 days.

Safari Bookshelf is an electronic reference library that lets you easily search thousands of technical books, find code samples, download chapters, and access technical information whenever and wherever you need it.

To gain 45-day Safari Enabled access to this book:

• Go to http://www.awprofessional.com/safarienabled
• Complete the brief registration form
• Enter the coupon code 6URG-5EGP-GFQ2-WHPY-TLZU

If you have difficulty registering on Safari Bookshelf or accessing the online edition, please e-mail customer-service@safaribooksonline.com.

Library of Congress Cataloging-in-Publication Data:
Buckley, Christian D.
    Implementing Rational Clear Quest : an end-to-end deployment guide / Christian D. Buckley,
Darren W. Pulsipher, and Kendall Scott.
        p. cm.
    Includes bibliographical references and index.
    ISBN 0-321-33486-8 (pbk. : alk. paper)
    1. Rational ClearQuest. 2. Software configuration management. 3. Computer software—
Development. I. Pulsipher, Darren W. II. Scott, Kendall, 1960– III. Title.
    QA76.76.C69B823 2006
    005.1—dc22   2006012464

All rights reserved. This publication is protected by copyright, and permission must be obtained from the publisher prior to any prohibited reproduction, storage in a retrieval system, or transmission in any form or by any means, electronic, mechanical, photocopying, recording, or likewise. For information regarding permissions, write to:

> Pearson Education, Inc.
> Rights and Contracts Department
> 75 Arlington St., Suite 300
> Boston, MA 02116
> Fax: (617) 848-7047

ISBN 0-321-33486-8
Text printed in the United States on recycled paper at Courier, in Stoughton, Massachusetts.
First printing, August 2006

Contents

xiv   Contents

Preface

Why This Book?

We attended the 2004 IBM Rational User Conference to promote our last book, *The Art of ClearCase Deployment* (Addison-Wesley, 2004), and to enjoy the warm and humid weather of Dallas, Texas. We set up shop next to the Pearson booth, only occasionally slipping away to engage in a game of multiplayer Quake at a booth across the way with a large display covering grid technology. Our book was selling well, and we were enjoying the interaction with the crowd. But one question kept popping up: "Does your book talk at all about Clear-Quest?"

Our answer was always apologetic: We discussed ClearQuest in the framework of the entire software configuration management continuum, but we did not specifically dive into the ClearQuest product or configuration. And yet the questions were persistent. People were obviously hungry for some formal content, for something more than the technical documentation available on the IBM website.

By the third day, we decided to talk to the Pearson team in attendance about the prospect of writing a ClearQuest book. We figured there had to be a project in the works somewhere, given the vast number of books related to change management already floating around out there. Apparently not. The Pearson team members were ecstatic, to put it mildly. They told us that there were no other books in the works and that they had been looking for someone to take the reins on the effort. To solidify our resolve, we also mentioned the possibility to several of the IBM marketing folks who had passed by throughout the week to check the status of our current book sales. They agreed that there was a huge demand for a book on the subject—so right then and there we agreed to take on the project. A few weeks later, our proposal had been accepted and a contract signed.

The Goal of This Book

Throughout our shared writing history (since 1997), we have always initiated our projects by first researching other authors and understanding what content has come before us and what questions have been left unanswered. For ClearQuest, there seemed to be a fairly large gap. Even the IBM website seemed to show a lack of content. Sure, there are plenty of training slides and technical manuals available online, and we have training materials from past versions and various external training companies. And during the past few months, there's been some effort to add articles outlining individual experiences integrating ClearQuest to various proprietary and mainstream applications. What was missing was a comprehensive view of ClearQuest that shows how it fits into the change management continuum.

Our intention with this book was to provide a solid roadmap for how to deploy ClearQuest, from the business justifications and issues, to the proper planning and design that will meet your current and longer-term business needs, down to the things you should consider around implementation of your design. ClearQuest is a flexible, dynamic application that can be modeled to fit your particular needs. The key to success is to properly plan your deployment, execute that plan, and provide adequate training for all users so there is acceptance of the new system and quantifiable benefits to your projects and products.

The goal of this book is to help the reader understand the actors, the business cases, and the *complete* problem domain before embarking on a defect-tracking implementation of any size. This book provides insight into the management issues, integration issues, and implementation issues surrounding the components of a ClearQuest deployment. The book also covers issues and tactical responses to implementing both small, team-based solutions as well as large, multisite deployments found in many of today's global enterprises.

ClearQuest is a natural partner to ClearCase for a robust configuration management solution. ClearCase provides the framework and the organization, while ClearQuest provides the interface for engineering, product management, field operations, and support to document and track defects, enhancements, issues, and documentation iterations.

Each chapter follows a logical flow, with the intent of providing actionable steps and relevant examples that you can use during your own planning. We offer practical guidelines for designing and deploying an end-to-end solution—all taken from our own experiences in building these kinds of solutions—and show how ClearQuest fits into the overall change management system. Each chapter contains relevant diagrams and visual examples to illustrate new concepts and ideas.

Our goal for *Implementing IBM Rational ClearQuest* is to present the material in a way that a broader group of project personnel can understand and use, while hopefully getting a better picture of how an end-to-end defect-tracking solution can enhance an organization's ability to address customer requirements more quickly. By helping a broader group of project players understand the change management continuum, we aim to help teams deliver better products, faster.

Our Writing Style

For those of you unfamiliar with our online articles or previous book, we are not your typical authors. Our writing style can be colloquial at times. We prefer to write in the same voice with which we work and consult; we present and teach on a regular basis, and we like to have fun with what we do.

The goal of our books is to ease the reader into the subject matter, most often through humor. The world does not need one more dry, difficult-to-consume technical book. While the subject matter in this book doesn't leave a lot of room for anecdotal stories, we've made some attempts at humor nonetheless.

We tend to follow a natural progression in our writing, moving the reader from broader concepts through to the more technical aspects of a ClearQuest deployment. In the early chapters, we start by making the business case for ClearQuest, moving you through some of the basic features to help you understand the full breadth of the solution, and then tackle the more complex issues toward the end. We want you to understand the actors, the use cases, and the *complete* problem domain before embarking on a change management implementation of any size.

Unlike other books in the broader category of software development best practices, this book will help you better understand how Clear-Quest fits into your change management solution by covering both strategic and tactical issues for deployment. Most chapters contain actionable steps that you can follow in your own planning efforts, along with relevant examples and plenty of screenshots.

Many of the diagrams, screenshots, and feature tables come from the IBM Rational ClearQuest manuals, available through purchase of the software. Some of the materials are also available online.

One other feature of this book is the association with the IBM developerWorks website. At the end of most chapters are links to relevant articles, training classes, and scripts to point you toward more detailed topics from IBM and other authors. The links are referenced by number throughout the chapter (A: article; T: training, S: script) in the order they appear.

Who Should Read This Book

Implementing IBM Rational ClearQuest is specifically targeted toward those readers who want to learn how to create an end-to-end change management solution using ClearQuest and how a robust defect-tracking system fits into the larger product development organization.

The book provides value propositions to three primary types of users:

1. The field engineer, who may access the system from within the office or while at a customer site

2. The manager in charge of change management (most likely the tool administrator), who will ultimately own and operate the system and ensure its integrity against the overall change management system

3. The senior manager or product manager, who relies on the information within the system to improve product design and response rates to customer requests and issues

The book assumes no particular knowledge of change management tools, object-oriented analysis and design, programming, or any modeling methodologies; however, it serves as both an introduction and a bridge, for example, to connection points with ClearCase.

The Structure of This Book

Chapter 1—Building and Maintaining the Feedback Loop
with Customers
One of the primary problems with most product development organizations is poor communication between development and

product management, and especially between the company and the customer. This chapter provides a case for building more robust communication channels between disparate groups.

Chapter 2—The Value Proposition
This chapter offers a synopsis outlining the value of ClearQuest. The chapter will help you understand the components of change management, define the value proposition within your own organization, and provide some suggestions on how to get buy-in from both your team and management.

Chapter 3—Selling Your Team on Change Management
Beyond the tool value proposition, this chapter outlines the nature of change requests and how to track them. It also provides a good overview of the role of various tools in the change management continuum.

Chapter 4—Moving Parts
This chapter presents the fundamentals of the ClearQuest architecture and the change request lifecycle. We explain the various ClearQuest components, basic installation, high-level administration and customization, and schema and database setup. We also show you how to work within ClearQuest Designer.

Chapter 5—Analyzing Your Company's Needs
Before you attempt to deploy any software application, you will want to adequately model your system. This chapter will help you define your ClearQuest actors, use cases, activity diagrams, workflow, and reports.

Chapter 6—Designing Your System
Following on the heels of analysis comes your system design. This chapter will assist you in your efforts to define classes, states and transitions, deployment diagrams, and your system-level design.

Chapter 7—Implementation: Schema and Database Design
Once your system has been designed, it is time to implement. This chapter walks you through the process of selecting your schema, defining your users and roles, creating groups, and setting up your database.

Chapter 8—Implementation: Customizing the Schema and Creating Hooks
With your core system established, you'll want to customize Clear-Quest to fit the nuances of your organization. This chapter will help you create your record type families, set field characteristics, define permissions, and perform custom scripting to individualize your solution.

Chapter 9—ClearQuest for Eclipse
This chapter contains everything you need to know to install, configure, and use the ClearQuest Eclipse plug-in.

Chapter 10—ClearQuest Integrations
This chapter provides an integration overview, including information about ClearQuest packages, Unified Change Management (UCM), and best practices for developing your own integrations.

Chapter 11—Deployment and Administration
With a focus on deployment activities, this chapter covers installation issues, database setup and configuration tasks, suggestions on testing and data backups, postinstallation issues, the always-bigger-than-it-seems data migration, and—of course—training your team.

Chapter 12—Multisite Development
What better way to wrap things up than to jump into what is possibly the most complex issue in the book: multisite deployment. This chapter reviews multisite design and management concepts such as synchronization, mastership, and how to resolve conflicts. Fun stuff.

About the Authors

Christian Buckley has a background in marketing and information technology. He has helped develop products and services for companies across a variety of industries, including software, financial services, supply chain, energy, and telecom. He has worked with some of the world's largest technology companies, including IBM, Microsoft, Hewlett-Packard, Visa, and Cadence Design Systems, among others, but has also participated in numerous startups as both advisor and team member.

An accomplished author and speaker, Christian has coauthored three books (with Darren) and published over 50 articles on topics ranging from software development and visual modeling to configuration management and project management. An author, speaker, and serial entrepreneur, Christian is the cofounder of the East Bay I.T. Group (http://www.ebig.org), a nonprofit technology forum serving the San Francisco East Bay. He has participated in the Global Grid Forum Marketing Awareness Council (GMAC) and is a member of the Product Development and Management Association (PDMA).

Christian holds an MBA in technology management and a bachelor of arts degree in marketing. He is currently pursuing a PhD in social informatics.

Darren Pulsipher has a rich background in software development and implementation, IT service and support, and strategic business operations. He is considered an expert in optimizing software development and improving management processes to decrease resource reliance while increasing product quality. As a result, he has been tapped on numerous occasions to consult with Fortune 500 companies on software development best practices. He holds 12 patents covering grid technologies, statistical graph modeling, and distributed fault tolerant systems. His 15 years of experience cover a wide range of industries, including network marketing, biotechnology, telecommunications, financial services, and electronic design automation. Much of this experience has been in the international arena with special focus in Europe and South America.

Representative of career accomplishments was his experience with Cadence Design Systems, the world's largest supplier of electronic design technologies and engineering services with annual revenues of $1.2 billion. As chief architect of grid strategies, Darren introduced tools and processes that reduced automated build and test system cycles by 60 percent. This resulted in a companywide savings of more than $15 million in hard costs, $30 million in soft costs, and more than 500,000 personnel hours.

Active in the international standards community, Darren has contributed to the Unified Modeling Language (UML) standard from the OMG, has been a primary contributor to the NPi standards organization, has presented at a number of conferences around the world, and been chair of three different groups in the Global Grid Forum (NPI-WG, JSDL-WG, and Policy-RG). He is also a member and contributor to the Global Grid Forum Marketing Awareness Council (GMAC). Darren holds an MBA in technology management and a bachelor of science degree in computer science.

Kendall Scott is a recognized expert in the UML. He has produced seven books related to the subject, including the best-selling *UML Distilled, Second Edition* (Addison-Wesley, 1999). He offers training and mentoring about the UML and the Rational Unified Process (RUP); his particular expertise lies in the gathering, analyzing, and negotiating of requirements using use cases and domain modeling.

1

Building and Maintaining the Feedback Loop with Customers

What is the financial value of customer feedback? Spend months or years building a product, most of that time planning for its deployment, release it with fanfare and all the good will you can muster—only to have customer after customer return your good deeds with comments, complaints, and suggestions for the *next* version. If it weren't for the customer, life would be a lot easier. Right?

Of course not. Nothing is further from the truth. Customers are the sole purpose for a company's existence; yet how well do we integrate their requirements and real-life experiences into how we build our products? Maybe your customers are internal. Be that as it may, your ability to manage their requests is just as critical as requests from external customers.

Many of us can relate to the all-too-familiar story of a lone project manager, sitting at a customer site on the opposite side of the country, waiting for a software vendor to call—a vendor whose application was integrated into his company's software solution—and needing to respond to a customer question about a piece of functionality that wasn't working as documented. As this project manager sat waiting for the phone to ring, his mind began to wander, and he found himself daydreaming about creating some kind of communication/teleportation technology that would allow him to reach through the telephone lines and smack the next person who had the nerve to tell him, "Well, we can't seem to recreate the problem over here. Can you tell me again what the problem is?"

How often have we heard that response from our IT teams or some other technical support person—a total disconnect from what the field support team and the customer are experiencing?

Well, the software vendor finally called the project manager back with the expected response: "Can you help us understand the problem? What is your user trying to do? We can't recreate your problem, and we need more information." After a redeye flight to the east coast from California, followed by six hours of user training and a poorly reheated fast-food lunchtime feast, the project manager in this story was on the edge.

Both the project manager and the vendor tried looking at the issue logically, but they obviously had different perspectives. The vendor's thought process was, "Just give me more information, and I'll run some test scripts. We'll try to figure out what is going on." On the other side, the project manager's thought process was, "If he doesn't understand the problem in the first place, how does he know he can't recreate it? What problem is he trying to resolve?"

Herein lies the fundamental breakdown among customers, the companies that serve them, and all of the organizations within the development food chain: There seems to be an endless volley among product management and engineering and engagement personnel to clarify exactly what the customer wants and needs, and what the development team can deliver. Most of us assume there is some kind of a "process" to handle the information being passed among the various organizations in the support chain, especially between our customers and any customer-facing organizations. In most companies, however, the "process" seems to consist of nothing more than an e-mail or a desperate phone call to the help desk.

Eye Protection Recommended

Of course, this all-too-familiar scenario has a domino effect.

The random e-mail or call into the help desk rarely satisfies the customer's desire to be heard. A customer who doesn't think his or her input was adequately prioritized will often contact one or two other people at the company. In some cases, the salesperson may enter the customer request into a bug/enhancement tool, as will one of the other people the customer contacts (possibly a customer service representative). The members of the QA team see these two new requests coming into the system from two different people, and they flag the development team for an update to each. These requests look similar, of course, but while they ultimately come from the same customer, they are identified as two different issues. Meanwhile, the salesperson has discussed the issue with a product manager and a buddy on the customer service team, and the customer service rep who was contacted directly by the customer has also shared this information with a second product manager. (Are you following this?)

Because their perspectives about the problem all came from different discussions, the salesperson, the two customer service people, and the product managers now have different understandings of the problem.

One of the product managers adds the issue to her next review meeting agenda, while the second product manager goes straight down to engineering to talk about short-term solutions. Based on that con-versation, engineering adds a small patch to the upcoming build schedule. Three days later, the salesperson logs into the bug/enhancement tool for an update. He doesn't see an update, so he contacts someone on the QA team, who refers him to engineering, where he learns that a patch is being applied in the next build. He then contacts the customer to give him the great news. A week later the build is completed, two weeks after that QA approves the release, and the customer logs on to the new build—only to find that the problem he reported is still there.

Ouch.

OK, while this account is largely a dramatization, this problem of miscommunication across the various layers of companies is all too real. Some of the finest, most well-organized teams have fallen into this communication trap. To overcome it, you need to automate, plain and simple.

It's the Tools, Stupid

Water flows down the path of least resistance. In our experience, so do communications between customer-facing groups and product development teams. We all hate to admit it, but when it comes to solving complex software problems or responding to detailed cus-tomer functionality requests, development teams usually do what it takes to get the product out the door—even if it means bypassing specific customer requests with the knowledge that they'll have to revisit the same problems later. This can be a financially risky deci-sion. Keeping development on schedule and receiving continual feedback from your customers (and providing information back to them) should not be mutually exclusive.

The key to resolving this issue is *knowledge*. Knowledge comes from understanding the root of the problem. To understand the root of the problem, you need to understand the business use case under which the problem was identified, and for that you need good documentation and a solid feedback loop between your customer, your customer-facing team, and your product development organization. Documentation is the key.

> The aspects of good documentation are simple: they must be clear, concise, consistent, and most importantly, they must deliver the expected results. This point deserves emphasis: it is one thing to create documentation that fulfills the technical requirements, but an entirely separate issue to create documentation that anticipates questions and provides solutions.[1]

But who has time for clear and concise documentation? Everyone, if you have the right tools and a pattern to follow. Put the tools in front of the people, and make them as simple as possible (the tools, not the people). The key to good documentation, as we all know, is accurate and thorough requirements. How do you get your globally dispersed sales team to input customer issues and requirements, you ask? Well, establishing this sort of two-way communication between your team and your customer is the point of this book.

Sure, there are a number of free tools available on the Internet, and many companies with time on their hands and money to burn have built their own solutions. However, we suggest using something a little more robust than the shareware or homebaked versions. Why? Security, for one. Most packaged solutions offer better control of access rights, roles and responsibilities, and data security. In addition, most off-the-shelf solutions offer a variety of integration and support options.

Figure 1–1 shows a simplified solution for a field team interacting with customers and a product team. The marketing requirements document (MRD) is typically the first pass on capturing a user's business requirements and may include simple workflow diagrams and logical data flow of key systems.

---

1. Christian Buckley and Darren Pulsipher, "Destroying the Tower of Babel: Communication Through Documentation," *Rose Architect Magazine*, January 1999:60–65.

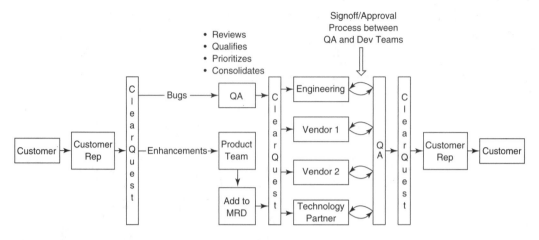

Figure 1–1   *Simplified communication model*

In any implementation, the steps need to be made clear to everyone within the feedback loop. Again, this is a simplified model, but it will help you understand the various options available to you through ClearQuest.

- Step 1: The customer contacts the appropriate customer representative with an issue or a suggestion. We suggest training everyone to get into the habit of pointing any user bug or enhancement request to someone on the team with ClearQuest access—or else make sure that anyone who comes into contact with a customer also has access to the tool, so you have one process for entering all issues. While people don't seem to mind passing this responsibility over to someone else, your best strategy may be to provide everyone in your organization with a login.

- Step 2: The customer rep documents the issue/suggestion, enters the information into the appropriate issue-tracking system—which, in this case, automatically logs an issue into the repository—and receives a tracking number. With a tight integration between ClearQuest and the issue-tracking system (which is customarily used and maintained by customer service), the rep can access the system at any point and get a status on this item. Each time the issue is edited (feedback provided), the issue-tracking system can be set up to receive an update, or an e-mail notice can be sent to the rep directly. (**Note:** While few companies will want customer service representatives to have access directly into a system that tracks engineering change requests, ClearQuest can be used this way.)

- Step 3: Issues are sent to QA, while enhancement requests are sent to product management. You don't have to set up your system like this, but in this model we wanted to make sure that the members of the product management team (our R&D shop) were responsible for all enhancement-related requests, so they could stay close to the customer usage patterns.

- Step 4: The issues/enhancements are reviewed (Does the request make sense?), qualified (Is this a valid request?), prioritized (Where does it fit into our current activities?), and consolidated (Do I have any similar requests already in the system?). ClearQuest is then updated with the appropriate feedback, which, in this model, automatically notifies the customer rep who entered the information. Again, you don't have to set up your system to notify the rep every time a change is made, but you might decide that you can better serve the customer by staying on top of any changes to the issue. You could just as easily log onto the system a dozen times a day.

- Step 5: Based on the update, the appropriate development organization receives the request and fits it into the development schedule. These teams do not receive the bug/enhancement until QA or product management flags it. You'll find this to be a great feature in itself. On previous systems, anyone who logged into the system, including the development team or an outside vendor, would have access to every single bug or enhancement that was logged into the tool. Not any more. Now they see only what you want them to see.

- Step 6: The development organization works with QA to test any new code. Build, test. Build, test.

- Step 7: Once approved, QA updates ClearQuest. Another great feature of ClearQuest: The issue isn't closed until QA—and QA alone—decides it's closed.

- Step 8: The customer rep is notified that the item has been closed. E-mail notifications are great.

- Step 9: The rep notifies the customer of the closure.

As with any tool, ClearQuest is not going to solve every problem, but if you don't have something similar in place, it's a great place to start. And, with integration into the full IBM Rational Software Development Platform, ClearQuest is one of the most powerful solutions on the market.

ClearQuest Roadmap

Based on this simple model, here is how we define the ClearQuest roadmap to success.

1. *Understand that information means business value.* Your product or service is what keeps your business running, and input from your customers is the lifeblood of that product or service. How you translate that customer feedback into your next version can mean the difference between version 2 and a decommissioned product.

2. *Train your customer-facing folks to properly capture the information.* Make yourself the documentation evangelist for your team or company. Advocate capturing requirements via entire sentences, as opposed to chopped-up fragments of what is generally regarded as written language. Persuade your team to break down each issue into logical chunks and to capture carefully the steps of the problem as well as the expected results. If you're documenting an enhancement request, include detailed use cases that explain how the customer would use the new functionality and why the request is im-

portant. This goes a long way when the product team is prioritizing issues. A well-detailed description will move items to the top of the list, believe us.

3. *Automate the mechanisms for entering information.* We've used both homegrown solutions and Internet freebies (Bugzilla), but we prefer ClearQuest because it offers more features and flexibility, and also because of its robust integration into ClearCase and other development lifecycle tools. Implement this tool in a way that allows key personnel to easily access and share information. This should be a no-brainer: Log in, define the appropriate component, prioritize your information, and then leave your data. The easier you make it, the likelier they are to use it.

4. *Set up a process for deciphering this information.* Once you have the information, what will you do with it? It's one thing to set up a vehicle for capturing and documenting customer information; it's another thing to get your product development team to respond, so that your sales team can provide timely feedback. Make the tool part of your daily/weekly/monthly process for reviewing issues and enhancements. Assign responsibility to some lucky product manager, and keep the repository updated.

5. *Assign tasks to necessary technical leads.* The product team has responded, and the appropriate technical lead—whether part of your internal engineering team or part of a third-party development organization—is automatically notified. Actually, this is a big incentive for most product management teams. They are acutely aware that the sooner they respond, the sooner the issue gets assigned to an engineer and moves off their own plate. How's that for motivation? Instead of the engineering team lead receiving e-mail notification for every single problem that comes across the product team, the system can organize and delegate based on components—and even based on severity.

6. *Update the repository at each step.* At each step of the process of solving your customer-defined issues, the repository is updated, the customer advocate has access to that information, and notifications are sent automatically. This is the key to cleaning up the entire process: Instead of pushing report after report across the organization, simplify, simplify, simplify. By following a defined process, and by using a single tool for managing this information, you'll have one version of the truth.

7. *Train customer-facing folks to log in and report back to customers.* Every Monday morning, as you begin your week, you know that you can log into the system and get the latest update on any issue or enhancement that was entered into the tool the previous week. How powerful is that?

Issue management is the fulcrum point to a successful software configuration management solution—and the key to issue management is setting up the proper lines of communication between your team and your customer.

The purpose of this chapter was to explain the high-level business value for ClearQuest, and hopefully we've achieved that. Now we're ready to jump into the meat of the program and show you how to get the most bang for your buck.

2

The Value Proposition

Change has a considerable psychological impact on the human mind. To the fearful it is threatening because it means that things may get worse. To the hopeful it is encouraging because things may get better. To the confident it is inspiring because the challenge exists to make things better.

King Whitney Jr.[1]

Consulting for startups (as opposed to large, bureaucratic firms) is a great experience for anyone interested in the creation of process. Small companies can be fast-paced and dynamic, or they can attempt to imitate larger companies with the belief that thinking big would somehow make them big. In the world of software configuration management (SCM), however, small companies are usually just like their larger and more revenue-rich counterparts, in that their systems can be a mess. Many firms look to automation and

---

1. As quoted in *The Wall Street Journal,* June 7, 1967.

more agile processes far down the road instead of right up front, when change is easier—and less expensive.

Change costs money. It costs time, and it takes people. So you'd think more companies would think a wee bit longer about the systems they put in place to manage their intellectual capital.

What is the value proposition for change request management software? Is it merely a way to document bugs reported by your test and engineering teams? How much have you thought about the overall process? Hopefully, in the pages to come, we'll make the case for ClearQuest.

Traditionally, smaller firms look for a change when the competitive solution they are using stops scaling to meet their needs. This is especially true of companies experiencing "repository corruption" problems. There's nothing like a corrupted repository that you can't recover from to send a company toward ClearQuest.

There is a natural progression in the growth and development of a software development team or a product management organization of any size. As your team develops and your customer base expands, the problems you will encounter, the sophistication required to manage these problems, and the scope of your solutions will become more and more complex. As a result, the tools required to manage these solutions need to be scalable and flexible.

This is the complexity that created modern change management solutions—tools created to manage the many user inputs and subsequent team outputs in an organized, efficient way. To successfully develop and deliver your own change management solution, you must look at the entire change management continuum and put in place the required tools and processes, which will allow your team to successfully perform change management.

The first step is software configuration management. We wrote an entire book on the topic (*The Art of ClearCase® Deployment*, Addison-Wesley, 2004). The second step is your defect-tracking solution.

Understanding the Components

What are change requests, and where do they fit into your change management model? When people talk about change request solutions, they are usually referring to the tools that manage defect tracking. However, this is just one aspect of the solution. If you step back and look at the bigger picture, you'll understand how a product like ClearQuest fits into the larger framework of how you communicate ideas across your organization. Consider these factors:

- *Identification*: identifying problems, questions, ideas
- *Control*: controlling workflow, providing visibility
- *Task prioritization*: prioritizing change requests and assignments
- *Status*: reporting status, changes, and their impacts
- *Audit*: tracking changes, seeing trends in data
- *Process*: ensuring that every request follows a particular lifecycle
- *Teamwork*: monitoring team interactions, lending a hand where needed

ClearQuest is a tool that supports all of these components. And now that you understand the components, how do you convince your team of the importance of taking your change request practices to the next level? Where do you start?

Change management, in general, is all about managing the increasing complexity of a project. Your team must be prepared to manage the complexities of an ever growing, always expanding list of customer demands, enhancements, and features. Also, failure to use input from outside is a common problem in software development. Many development organizations treat the tools they use as part of a self-contained environment for generating and resolving issues. This is a problem because valuable input can also come from outside of the development team. ClearQuest is a tool that will provide you with links into the internal and external customers who will drive the direction of your products.

Participation by other user communities, including sales, marketing, management, and the customer, only improves the process and increases the value of the system to the company. An isolated, developer-centric view can cause these applications to become disposable and transient, thus never becoming part of the larger change management ecosystem.

With this engineering-centric view of the world, the other difficulty is that these systems do not encompass the larger business processes, which limits the value to the organization and prevents further expansion of processes and the formalization of a broader culture for tracking change requests. An enterprise change request solution must have robust core capabilities that adhere to a common workflow, while retaining flexibility in areas that allow it to be easily adaptable to the needs of multiple project stakeholders.

You need to understand how change requests fit into your current company workflows, how they fit into the mechanics of your version control system, and how they interact with the myriad of user and developer tools and systems. The questions you need to answer as you move forward include: What are your current processes? How strictly are they adhered to? How will a more dynamic change request solution change the way your team works? How will you administer your users? How will you prioritize your enhancements?

A critical aspect of implementing any kind of change management solution is understanding all of the actors of the system: Who needs access, and where are they located? You may all be centrally located in one office now, but what are your company's plans for growth? Will you outsource any of your development, thus requiring coordination with outside groups? Are your primary users "power users" who are more technically savvy and therefore will want more interaction with their change requests, or will all customer input come through your own help desk organization?

Answering these questions will help you define the actors of your system, and the actors will help you better refine your CM solution and, in turn, define how ClearQuest should be refined or expanded. In Chapter 5, we will teach you how to further analyze your current system and start the planning process for your new ClearQuest deployment. First, however, it's worthwhile to understand the value proposition for deploying ClearQuest.

Defining Your Value Proposition

Consumers all want technology that is faster, smaller, and more efficient. Arguably, the same trend is happening in our expectations in the workplace: As technology projects become more complex, we demand tools that are faster, less invasive to our existing systems, and more efficient.

Fortunately, change management systems are moving in the same direction as our expectations. They can be a powerful asset to increasing communication, productivity, and quality through process automation and integration of the tools that most engineering groups use today. Implementing some kind of CM solution will organize your development efforts around solid and repeatable processes—and by helping your team to more effectively prioritize and manage the product development lifecycle, you are more likely to meet your customers' needs.

[A.2.1] However, one big concern of every development organization is the impact of adding a new tool or process to the existing workload and development schedule. It's easy to get carried away with any new tool deployment. You know the basic features, and you probably have a rough idea of how the tool will fit into your company processes. For others, though, there may still be some footwork to be done to convince a manager or an executive that yet another tool will do *anything* to make your team—or the company—more productive at product development.

What is the value proposition for your engineers? What is the value proposition for your testers? What is the value proposition for your CM managers? What is the value proposition for your field reps? And, most importantly, what is the value proposition for your executive team?

The typical software development organization has a variety of requirements management, enhancement prioritization, and defect-tracking systems, all of which could have increased value or be improved in the following areas:

- Business value
- Developer-centricity
- Use within business processes
- Value to management

Selling the ClearQuest value into your organization can be a simple proposition, following one or more of these value themes. Or it could be like pulling teeth—depending on your current toolset (Are we duplicating current functionality?), the amount of pain your company may be going through (Will this help us respond more quickly to user demands?), or how quickly your management team responds to new ideas (We have a development team?).

The requirements for your solution may include any or all of the following:

- Integrated workflow and methods for notification
- Quick deployment to new teams or other user groups
- Streamlined and simple user interfaces that can leverage existing processes
- Easy-to-use APIs to support integration with compatible systems, such as customer relationship management (CRM) help desk, or other CM systems
- The ability to gauge objective, real-time project status

ClearQuest enables team members to look at the record of a change request at any time and know what has been done on it, what tasks remain to be done on it, who is working on it, when it is expected to be fixed, and so forth. Team members can stay informed about the status of a change request as work on it progresses. This can, for example, help project managers make more informed decisions about project timelines and resource allocation.

It doesn't make much sense for us to try to identify every scenario you might encounter in selling ClearQuest into your organization, or that magic combination of requirements that will make your management team suddenly embrace the idea of adding another tool to the system. That kind of deep introspection would require a much longer book (and, to be honest, it would also cut into our consulting margins). You'll just have to do some investigating on your own and come up with the best way to present the idea to your management chain.

What we *can* do, however, is give you a solid overview of what ClearQuest can do for your company so you can figure out which benefits best apply to your company's pains.

Generally, defect- and change-tracking tools primarily benefit development, project management, and production by helping team members do the following.

- Avoid duplicating efforts.
- Prioritize change requests so the most important issues are resolved first.
- Keep the development process on the right track by enabling team members to monitor project status as the project evolves.
- Improve the level of teamwork among all participants.
- Resolve differences before they become serious problems.
- Establish a mechanism for constant product improvement.

Think about how these things can affect your current team and customer interactions, in terms of both improving communication of issues and ideas and providing much-needed visibility into the change process.

The IBM Rational website contains more specific information about ClearQuest features, including how it does the following:

- Provides activity-based change and defect tracking

- Manages all types of change requests, including defects, enhancements, issues, and documentation changes, with a flexible workflow process

- Enables easy customization of defect and change request fields, processes, user interfaces, queries, charts, and reports

- Provides predefined configurations and automatic e-mail notification and submission out of the box

- Works with Rational ClearCase to provide a complete SCM solution

- Provides "design once, deploy anywhere" capabilities that automatically propagate changes to any client interface (Windows, Linux, UNIX, web)

- Offers deep integration with IBM WebSphere Studio, Eclipse, and Microsoft .NET IDEs for instant access to change information

- Supports Unified Change Management (UCM) for proven change management process support

- Scales easily to support projects regardless of team size, location, or platform

ClearQuest has been included and integrated in the IBM Rational Suite and the IBM Rational Team Unifying Platform for lifecycle change management.

ClearQuest MultiSite, which provides the ability to manage geographically distributed activities, is available separately or as part of Rational ClearCase Change Management Solution Enterprise Edition. Key features of this product include the following:

- Enabling of replication of schema repositories and user databases across multiple geographic locations

- Saving of time and network resources with efficient transmittal of only incremental changes that appear in Rational ClearQuest project repositories

- Automatic resends of information during network failures

- Recovery of repositories in the event of system failure

[A.2.2] See the IBM Rational ClearQuest product website for more information.

Getting Team Buy-In

So, we'll ask the questions one more time: What is the value proposition for your engineers? What is the value proposition for your testers? What is the value proposition for your CM managers? What is the value proposition for your field reps? And, most importantly, what is the value proposition for your executive team? We've discussed what a tool like ClearQuest can do for your company, but how do its features address the questions and concerns of each of these user groups?

- **Engineers**
  If your engineering team does not already have some kind of change request toolset in place, it will be more than willing to implement ClearQuest—especially if the members of the team are already using ClearCase. ClearQuest will allow them to better define, respond to, and track change requests coming into the system. On the other hand, developers themselves

are notorious for resisting process implementations because they often perceive process as extraneous overhead that drains their productivity. If a development team is required to use ClearQuest without answering basic questions (e.g., Why not use Bugzilla or another open source solution? Why do we need SCM at all?), it will most likely do so grudgingly. In most cases, only after ClearQuest has been shown to improve their productivity over other options will the team members embrace it.

- **Testers**
  Testers are a difficult challenge. They are continually under pressure to deliver high-quality applications, with shrinking development and deployment schedules impacting their ability to reflect much on new tools. Add to that geographically distributed organizations, limited resources, and high turnover rates for skilled employees, and you can see how application testing can be a rough place to initiate change. However, faced with the reality of having to do more with less, juggle multiple projects, and manage diverse and distributed project teams, you definitely have the attention of testing management. Many organizations are implementing automated test management tools to help centralize, organize, prioritize, and document their testing efforts, and ClearQuest answers many of their needs.

- **CM Managers**
  This is an easy sell, in our estimation. ClearQuest fits right into the IBM Rational software configuration management model and extends the capabilities that CM managers already administer.

- **Field Reps**
  [A.2.3] Using ClearQuest's web or e-mail interface provides technicians, engagement personnel, and other field representatives with a way to feed their input back into the system. In most cases, these people are providing the most relevant data to the development organization, as they are the ones working

directly with the customers. They understand the problems being encountered, and they will appreciate a more formal, automated method for inputting change requests. There may be an intermediate step between reps and ClearQuest—such as a formal issue-tracking system—but ultimately the feedback should reach ClearQuest.

- **Executive Team**
  Buy-in from management is the key to getting any large organizational initiative approved and, in most companies, to implementing any kind of change that will reach across multiple organizations. One problem with defect-tracking systems is a general lack of perceived value for management: Because the executives don't see the value in the contributions of such systems, it can be difficult to get them to participate in the process. You need to show CxOs that ClearQuest helps them by:

  - Accelerating the development cycle by helping them more effectively manage and control change, helping them get products to market faster—thereby giving them a competitive edge in the marketplace
  - Enabling them to allocate resources more intelligently, by getting real-time project metrics
  - Enabling their teams to communicate and collaborate better, getting more done in less time

All of these effects impact the bottom line, and this is what is most important to CxOs.

One of the strengths of ClearQuest is the data that comes out of it, from reports and charts to raw metrics, plus the ability to pull the data into some kind of management dashboard. Ultimately, the most important factor for selling to management is the visibility into customer issues. Instead of a screened summary of issues, management can get direct access into real change requests and watch as they are defined, prioritized, and resolved.

There are two other important user groups you should also consider when selling ClearQuest into your organization. Part of the extended product development organization, they serve a vital link to customers and industry—a link critical to keeping your technology on top of the competition.

- **Help Desk**
  A variety of issue-tracking tools have been developed specifically for help desks and support organizations, but it's important to provide help desk managers with access to ClearQuest. At a minimum, you should provide each help desk manager with access, allowing him or her to input change requests coming directly from customers and also ideas and enhancements based on the manager's constant interactions with users. Preferably, you will automate this process and provide some kind of integration between the help desk systems and ClearQuest to allow for automatic change request generation; this will relieve your help desk managers from all of the double entry.

- **Product Managers**
  It's always amazing to see how disconnected product management can be from the development side of so many businesses. Here are individuals who are central to the planning and development of new directions for your products or software, yet they are too often located away from engineers. In some organizations they do not have access to the wealth of information coming in from testing, the help desk, and the field reps. By including product managers in the loop, you will directly impact the quality of your future products.

Understanding Target User Scenarios

What's the real business purpose for defect tracking, anyway? Why not manage all of your customer and testing team inputs through e-mail, or build some kind of internal portal where it's all just tracked through spreadsheets or constantly updated PowerPoint presentations?

It's astounding to what ends a company will go to create a tracking solution instead of going out and buying something off the shelf that addresses that particular pain. It's also amazing how far people will test the limits of their freeware and stretch the many manual processes supporting their hybrid, homebaked solutions before coming to the conclusion that they need a more robust, versatile solution for their change request needs.

We all recognize that there is a natural progression in the growth and development of a development team and their tools, but what are the leading scenarios to indicate that your team is ready to roll out ClearQuest?

It's one thing to propose a new tool based on its functionality and cost points. This may sway some managers, but a better approach is to help your executive team understand the various pain points your development, support, and field teams are experiencing, and how a product such as ClearQuest can help alleviate that pain.

The following list is not all-inclusive, but it should provide some identifiable scenarios to help you make your case.

- *You have recently expanded your development organization by opening a regional office in another country.* We live in an increasingly global development community, so multisite development capability has become critical to many companies. We now have to manage around offshore development teams, onshore outsourced components, and the regular occurrence of mergers and acquisitions, layering onto this fun mix of confusion and technology sometimes not-so-complementary products and services. By tracking change requests in a single place, multiple geographical locations can work together very closely to prioritize work, delegate responsibility, and resolve issues that affect multiple product lines.

- *You spend more time adding features to your homemade solution than you do building and testing your product.* Build a proprietary solution, and you will own support, development, and expansion of that solution. Every time your business processes change, a new tool is added, or problems pop up, you will find yourself navigating a vast web of scripts and quickly concocted add-ons to make up for the lack of onboard functionality in your toolset. ClearQuest is a commercial product and has the support, compatibility, and feature set you will need to accomplish your tasks; it will provide your organization with a robust change management solution. Most freeware doesn't come close to ClearQuest in terms of functionality and integration.

- *A product manager asks you to prioritize issues based on responses from your key customers.* What kind of data can you currently provide to your management team or product development organization? More importantly, can they access your current system and get the information themselves? The power of a total change management solution, which consists of configuration management coupled with defect tracking, is in the decision support capabilities it enables. Product managers envision future products based on input from customers and industry; their ability to capture data trends in defects, enhancement requests, and other input from the field, and from development, is instrumental in their ability to stay ahead of the competition.

- *You lost three weeks of work because the machine on which you were developing bit the dust.* With some freeware tools and with the proprietary solutions, how secure is your data? Has your system been architected to a centralized model, allowing for proper backup?

- *You need to control the content of your product, and you want to harvest the low-hanging fruit first.* ClearQuest includes an integration with software configuration management systems, such as IBM Rational's ClearCase. These integrations also help project managers control the content that gets into the product releases. By expanding the number of participants in the definition and resolution of change requests to include product management input, you will be able to make more informed decisions about the priority of product features.

- *Your IT budget was just increased, and it's "spend it or lose it."* OK, all of us experience this at least once. Departmental funding has grown, and suddenly you're flush with the cash you need to expand your system capabilities. Where can you get the most bang for your buck? As we tried to illustrate in Chapter 1, money spent on expanding your feedback loops among engineering, the testing team, the product management team, and the customer is money well spent.

Again, these examples don't include every single scenario for your use of ClearQuest, but they should cover most of your issues and help you make the case to your management team that a product like ClearQuest will help fill a gap in your current change management solution.

> He who every morning plans the transaction of the day and follows out that plan, carries a thread that will guide him through the maze of the most busy life. But where no plan is laid, where the disposal of time is surrendered merely to the chance of incidence, chaos will soon reign.[2]

The Value of Improving Quality

[A.2.4] Rolling out a change request solution and integrating that tool into your overall change management solution is not a task to be taken lightly. Don't fall into the trap of launching a large process or standards initiative without having a clear understanding of how much time and effort it will actually take. It's also important to understand the time frame for receiving benefits from the new system and to set expectations appropriately. A full implementation

---

2. Victor Hugo, *The Hunchback of Notre Dame*, 1831.

includes installation, refinement of process, fine-tuning of the system, and a lot of user training. Too many efforts fall short because there isn't a clearly defined owner or evangelist. A successful implementation requires a steady hand and close adherence to company standards.

It's a fact that most organizations depend on the CM team for information, guidance, and process. Configuration management can play an important role in how your company monitors and improves the quality of your products through process improvement, metrics, and cross-team communication. ClearQuest, as with most change request solutions in general, is unique in how it is viewed by development organizations because it fills a need that runs across many teams, and it also serves as the backbone to communication between company and customer, product management and testing group. That's a powerful incentive for all organizations within your company to make sure that this product is rolled out successfully.

How do you quantify quality? Well, you can't (at least in the world of software development). As a consumer, you know quality when you see it. When your head is down and you're trying to get a product out the door, though, it's easy to miss unless it's a company or team best practice. It's a difficult proposition to sell your management team on a product that improves overall quality when what they want to see is an improvement to the bottom line. However, you *can* illustrate business value and how ClearQuest fills gaps across the entire company. You *can* show them the power of developer-centricity and the ability to more easily extend process across geographic boundaries. You *can* sell them on integration with current business processes and how ClearQuest fits into the overall change management continuum. You *can* position the increased visibility and decision support capability as a value to management.

And finally, you can show them that ClearQuest helps improve the bottom line. It enables companies to use the resources it has more efficiently, helps team members communicate better—thereby improving their productivity—and helps accelerate time-to-market. All of these factors are excellent business/financial reasons for implementing ClearQuest.

developerWorks Links

A.2.1	http://www-128.ibm.com/developerworks/rational/library/3781.html
A.2.2	http://www-128.ibm.com/developerworks/rational/library/4606.html
A.2.3	http://www.redbooks.ibm.com/abstracts/SG246399.html?Open
A.2.4	http://www-128.ibm.com/developerworks/rational/library/4995.html

3

Selling Your Team on Change Management

One of the most difficult aspects of building solid technology is setting up the lines of communication in your organization. No out-of-the-box solution will solve all of your organization's data and communication needs. However, a good policy is to err on the side of too much information, and subsequently pare back your tools and systems as your organization becomes more consistent in its delivery of your product, as teams adjust to working together, and as your overall business processes become more refined.

One software company's experience may sound familiar to some. It was a growing company with a largely development-centric management team. They were growing quickly, finding it more and more difficult to manage their development efforts on the small, home-grown system they had created. They decided to make the move to ClearCase for source code and product management. For issue management, the company had already deployed a support desk application, and they made a weak attempt to use this platform to solve all of their internal issue-tracking needs. The tools did not map to their existing processes very well, and they had to be supplemented by an increasingly overwhelming number of management and team meetings to keep the flow of information up to date across the development organization and also to help prioritize rapidly changing product enhancements and issues. In short, the attempted solution wasn't working.

After the organization started using ClearCase to solve some of the major support system issues, someone on the development team read in the ClearCase product information and licensing agreement that the company had also bought ClearQuest software. With the software paid for, and an obvious need to put a more robust defect- and enhancement-tracking solution in place, the management team authorized an engineer to spend half of his time to roll out a solution. Within two days, he had the tool running and mapped to some of the more critical product workflows. Over the course of the next month, the solution was integrated with the help desk application, and the product management team was plugged into the system. This important step ensured that all participants in the product development lifecycle—not just development and quality assurance— were part of the system.

Our point in sharing this experience? ClearQuest is a tool that can be deployed very quickly, and it adds value immediately. Any new application can seem daunting, but quickly looking at ClearQuest's primary functions and navigating through the main user controls will illustrate how user-friendly this application really is. However, the first step is to know and understand the basics.

If you're going to sell your management team—or your development organization—on the decision to deploy ClearQuest, you need to have a good understanding of how change requests will work within your organization and how ClearQuest will interact with current and future systems.

Understanding Change Requests

Not every ClearQuest user works in a software development organization, so a change request should not be equated to just a software bug. A change request could take the form of a defect report, an enhancement request, or a feature request. Defects could be bugs, design flaws, or reports of irregular behaviors inside an application or on a product. Enhancements could be internal or external requests for changes to a product to modify an incomplete operation, fulfill a user expectation, or help bridge a functional gap in a product or solution. Finally, a feature request could be something that takes an existing product in a whole new direction, creates a new application, or brings to light a new technique or approach.

Everyone who interacts with a product or application should be viewed as a customer, and all customers should have some kind of mechanism in place to provide feedback. All customers want to see their requests answered by your company and hopefully incorporated into future product plans.

Tracking Change Requests

Change requests don't just happen in a vacuum. They must be reviewed, prioritized, tracked, and executed.

Most companies have developed lengthy and detailed processes to receive and handle change requests in a timely fashion. Each type of change request should be defined in a standardized way; in an Internet world, users and customers expect a quick response to any request. Your process should categorize change requests, which will help establish a timely and consistent model for your responses.

A centralized change- and defect-tracking tool allows your company to work together to resolve issues and decreases the chances of overlap by different teams. It also provides a critical resource for determining metrics against your defects and enhancement databases.

By organizing your processes around defect and change requests, you'll see an improvement in many aspects of the product development lifecycle. A simple process would include the following steps.

1. Change requests are made for a product or project.

2. These requests are organized in one central location.

3. A formal change review process is established; this process specifies the proper actions to take for each request type.

4. Managers assign tasks appropriately and schedule tasks for their resolution.

5. The tracking process should be reviewed regularly and refined as necessary to keep up with the growth and expansion of the company.

Is It the Process or the Tools?

ClearQuest is a valuable beast of burden. As the IBM Rational marketing team expressed in its online promotional materials, by using ClearQuest—in conjunction with ClearCase—as a complete CM solution, you can relate changes made to software components and web content to the requests that triggered those changes. In essence, you'll be not only taking advantage of the full potential of your ClearCase software's capabilities but also enhancing your entire change management solution.

It could be that your existing tools are inefficient, and you need something more robust and capable of deep integration with other tools—or it could be that your process has become more complex with the maturity of your company or organization, and you need ClearQuest for its flexibility and, well, integration. We're assuming you've personally already been sold on the benefits of ClearQuest and have deployed it or are planning to deploy it as your software development team's default defect- and enhancement-tracking tool. That's really only the first step. Where do you go from there? Well, have you thought about how this tool will integrate with the rest of your operations?

Have you looked at the possible use cases for expanding the tool across your various business processes or for integrating it with your other applications? Before you answer yes, answer the following questions.

- Have you looked at the business needs for extending your issue/enhancement-tracking capabilities?

- Have you queried your developers, your project managers and analysts, or even your customers about their needs?

- Have you made plans for integrating ClearQuest with your other Rational tools? (They don't call it a "tool suite" for nothing, you know.)

- Have you looked outside of the Rational tool suite for tool and process integration opportunities?

When you want to expand this important functionality, it's usually best to start with some kind of business needs analysis. Maybe you work for an organization that is small enough or flexible enough to make software purchases and integration decisions without a bunch of hoopla, but most of us need to justify the time and expense. We need to provide upper management with a strong value proposition for the time and energy it will take to link these tools and processes together into one seamless, kick-butt system.

In Chapter 1, we walked through a customer engagement scenario that was a concatenation of experiences from several past projects. We relived some very painful moments to illustrate a point: Working without *some* kind of communication infrastructure between engagement personnel and the development organization can be a competitive disadvantage. We'll even take that one step further by insisting that if you don't provide tools for rapid problem resolution, you are doing a disservice to your customers.

Follow the logic. Projects go awry—no one will argue that Murphy's Law lives and breathes in the software development world, probably more so than in just about any other industry. Given that, it should be the goal of your company to optimize the tools and processes for servicing your customers, so that you can spend the majority of your time managing the external influences that impact your projects instead of fighting your own internal processes.

The goal of the first two chapters was to establish the business need for an engagement-to-development communication solution. We're big believers in making communication from the field back to the home base as simple as possible—but it also has to be two-way. In other words, as important as it is to feed information into the organization, it's equally important to pull information back out of the organization and provide timely and accurate updates to your customers.

Selling ClearQuest into your own organization follows many of these same business justifications: the need to build lines of communication with your customers, to adopt tools that fit into your existing processes while providing new functionality, and to integrate Clear-Quest with other tools within the Rational Suite and with other back-end systems.

During uncertain economic times, everything you do must provide short-term value to the business and the customer base. Even if your company is seeing double-digit growth and record revenue, it's still important to understand how your tool and process improvements will affect your organization's ability to serve your internal and external customers. And to understand these impacts, you need to understand the business use cases and value proposition of any project you undertake—especially projects that expand your toolset and impact the way you work.

So, what functionality does ClearQuest provide? For starters, it acts as a buffer to your team and your project, collecting change and enhancement requests from the field and helping your team evaluate and prioritize this information before this data impacts your project. ClearQuest also allows you to manage various request types differently, enabling specialized workflows to handle each. ClearQuest has been referred to as a *clearinghouse* that collects and filters data, letting you control the effects of that data on your project.

As change requests are entered into the tool—requests that are accepted or rejected and subsequently drive your new system functionality—it is critical to be able to track these change requests, to understand their points of origin, and to provide feedback to the functionality requestor.

Integration is the key to getting the full value out of ClearQuest. Integration between a change request management tool and a configuration management tool, such as ClearCase, is the first step in unleashing the potential of the full Rational suite of tools. Add onto this with a requirements management tool (IBM Rational RequisitePro) and, for example, web-based build-reporting mechanisms, and you'll be better prepared to track exactly what features were committed and when those features have completed their build cycle. Most importantly, this network of tools allows you to more rapidly deliver against your stakeholder expectations, which will help you ensure that by the time you deliver your product, it still provides value.

There are numerous options for integration, including linking to project management tools, adding a third-party build-reporting tool, or even hooking the system into your customer relationship management system. However, the meat and potatoes of ClearQuest integration are configuration management and requirements management. Here's a quick overview of the overall value of integrating these tools.

- **Configuration Management**
  If you use ClearQuest with ClearCase, you get a single, comprehensive platform for efficient web content and code management. With regard to Unified Change Management (UCM)

functionality, ClearQuest gives you scheduled activities, assignment, state, user-defined fields and forms, and roles and security. ClearCase, on the other hand, provides all new objects and UCM infrastructure, projects, components, baselines, change sets, streams, and so forth.

With access to this centralized repository, team members can work on related development activities simultaneously. They can check out parts of the project and work on them in their own private, highly flexible workspaces. Content managers, for example, can either view their work in relation to changes made by other team members or keep it isolated until all changes are complete and checked in. Any changes would be tracked within the system, and notifications would go out to the stakeholders automatically.

The combination of these two tools provides a great advantage to distributed teams, content developers, designers, web developers, and software engineers. They will all have access to the artifacts stored in the Rational ClearCase database, as well as a unified defect- and change-tracking system. How powerful is that?

- **Requirements Management**
  [A.3.1] In the beginning, there were requirements. Let's not forget that so many of our products are created from the ideas of wonderful people—project managers, technical writers, and analysts. In addition to build environments, modern software development tools and practices involve many other types of electronic artifacts: visual models, source code, binaries, documentation, test scripts, images, web content, and, of course, requirements.

  Because ClearCase and ClearQuest can be fully integrated with Rational RequisitePro, your team leads can always have a view of the big picture and a clear understanding of what they need to control. Think about the management of your website. Content is constantly being added or changed, and it can be difficult to manage this level of change activity. With RequisitePro integration, you'll have instant access to precise specifications about what will or will not be in the website, and ClearQuest will update the critical stakeholders automatically whenever a change is made.

[S.3.1] On the question of when to use RequisitePro versus ClearQuest, it really just depends on how your organization uses these tools. RequisitePro is generally used for enhancements only, as more of a strategic tool, while ClearQuest is for day-to-day issue and bug tracking, and feeding those inputs into the development and product teams.

One of the major difficulties within most development organizations can be integration of the applications and business processes of various teams. Tools used by development teams may not connect with the tools in use by the product management team, the support team, and the field services team. What are the primary systems you may want to consider when planning your integrations and making your case to management about the value of ClearQuest and a total change management solution? Here are some heavy hitters.

- **E-mail**
  This one is a no-brainer. By adding the built-in facility of e-mail notification, you have the ability to send messages to anyone affected by an event in ClearQuest. When an engagement manager enters an enhancement request from the field into the system, for example, the system can automatically notify the appropriate engineer who is assigned to that feature set of your product. Once that enhancement has been accepted or rejected—or, better yet, once a specific defect has been resolved—the engagement manager is notified immediately, which allows him or her to get right back to that customer. This combination of tools will help your team stay apprised of all significant events in the lifecycle of the defect.

  Web-based build-reporting tools, many available through Rational partners and third-party vendors, can also be linked to your e-mail system to provide automated notifications, which will subsequently increase the value of your system.

- **Support Desk Applications**

  For those of you unfamiliar with this arena, a good example is Remedy (http://www.bmc.remedy.com). Remedy is a widely used incident management solution, used primarily by help desks, that allows organizations to quickly and effectively respond to end-user or infrastructure events or problems. Remedy offers automated workflows that are designed to respond to end-user requests according to parameters defined by shared service level agreements.

  The power of Remedy is in the problem management facilities, which provide root cause analysis of high-impact issues, spanning multiple incidents. This allows support teams to identify when and how errors occur, to see the trends of these issues across time, and to provide direct access to specific solutions or information in a company knowledge database based on the company's problem resolution workflow.

  The disconnect between customer-facing teams and your development team can sometimes be huge. On one side, you have your support desk and field personnel using a product such as Remedy to track incidents; on the other side is your development team using ClearQuest for defect tracking—and there's no way to track issues across the two systems. A product such as Remedy, in many cases, is your primary support desk application, helping the company track all new user deployments, for example. ClearQuest, on the other hand, will most likely be the primary system used by the internal development organization to track specific product enhancements, defects, and new requirements, with direct integration with your overall configuration management tool, which is most likely ClearCase.

  Without integration of these two systems, issues tracked within Remedy have to be reentered into ClearQuest manually. If an issue is one that the development team needs to be aware of, the process relies on someone in the support area entering the issue into both systems; the issue is thus generally tracked by spreadsheet or on handwritten notes, depending on the support representative. And then, once a problem is resolved, there's no automated method for getting a technical update in ClearQuest back into Remedy so that the customer making the request knows the status. Once again, it's up to the support person to check the status within ClearQuest and add the update within Remedy, and/or notify the customer directly. On top of it all, product managers—and therefore company executives—have no visibility into the full range of issues and requests coming from the customer. Without this visibility, they will have a difficult time understanding customer usage patterns and knowing where to make changes or upgrades to improve the product they're building.

Both Remedy and ClearQuest have their benefits and, of course, their target audiences. While some teams may find that ClearQuest alone meets the needs of their entire organization, when ClearQuest is customized through integration with other critical back-end systems, the result is increased management and development team visibility across these systems.

- **Decision Support Systems**
  Some companies with a product development focus have created or deployed tools that allow them to better track requirements and product features throughout the development lifecycle. The basic concept here is that seeing the data behind your requirements—which customers are making the requests, how each product feature affects the product line (and company) profit/loss statement, and what can be delivered within specified timelines—helps a company make better decisions about its products and services and better serve the needs of its customer base.

ClearQuest fits in with this category of application, although it may be viewed differently by some organizations depending on their tools and processes. The fact that ClearQuest can be flexibly applied to these systems to fill in the functionality gaps, and also to integrate these tools with the software development team more effectively, provides yet another benefit for deploying this tool.

Many companies suffer from a lack of visibility across organizational boundaries, affecting their ability to quickly capture, prioritize, and respond to industry or customer demands. Understanding the shared artifacts of your key applications—in this example, requirements and enhancement requests—is just the first step in designing an efficient and integrated management solution.

How and What to Plug and Play

[A.3.2] ClearQuest offers plenty of options for integration, but there isn't any comprehensive guide to which tools will work best for your own company and within the boundaries of your existing processes. The other concern is that many of your critical applications may not be exactly plug-and-play.

As part of your planning process, you should investigate what has been done before as far as ClearQuest integrations and where you may be breaking some new ground. Most companies do some level of e-mail integration, and you can rest assured that there are plenty of online resources for integrating ClearQuest with ClearCase and other leading software configuration management solutions. But what about your eight-year-old requirements management application that everyone just loves and doesn't want to give up? What about that new support desk system the company just went over budget on because it was the latest and greatest?

You can start by digging through the IBM developerWorks website (a fantastic resource, we might add) for white papers, manuals, and related articles. The website recommends the manual *Installing Rational Suite* (also available in an electronic version on the *Rational Solutions for Windows Online Documentation* CD) and the Rational Suite Release Notes. You can search the support documentation online at http://www.ibm.com/.

As of this writing, Rational is still working to pull together an all-inclusive collection of integration materials (a topic we cover in Chapter 10). While these materials do not focus entirely on Clear-Quest, you'll find some good information on how to get started. Articles such as "Leveraging Points of Integration in Rational Suite: An Introduction" by Brenda Cammarano can be found online through developerWorks. While it's just an overview of content being developed, her article covers the basic architecture of the Suite integrations.

As Brenda outlines, integrations of ClearQuest with other tools from the Rational Suite can help team members do the following:

- Easily transform requirements into test cases and automatically verify functionality

- Append test results to bug reports, thereby saving hours of attempts to recreate user errors

- Assess the integrity of application architectures early in the project lifecycle

- Design and code an application based on system requirements

What is the value of integrating these tools? Well, the advantages are automation and less administration, which will allow you to spend more time developing your products and meeting your customers' needs. In short, your development team can maximize its productivity while unifying its subteams, and the customer-facing folks can be more responsive.

Just to give you a quick perspective on how the tools are actually linked: It's all done through the Rational Extensibility Interface. The extensible architecture built around this interface exposes an internal structure that allows the customer to deploy on different computers (or domain servers) within the structure's network. It provides an opportunity to optimize network traffic as well as access to artifacts. Figure 3–1 shows the logical relationships within this architecture.

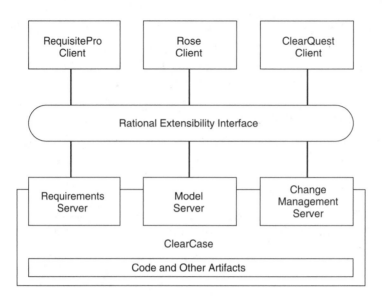

Figure 3–1 *Rational extensibility architecture*

Obviously, this diagram doesn't cover all of the products in the suite, but the way the tools connect through the extensibility interface remains the same.

This architecture also separates the user interface of each tool from the application-server functionality that's responsible for semantic understanding and persistent storage of the artifacts appropriate to the tool. This structure optimizes each domain server, where a domain server stores and manages data for requirements, visual models, test assets, and change requests within the project. By separating the user interface from server functionality, and then implementing a common Rational Suite Extensibility API across all of these servers, Rational provides a unique and powerful architecture for a project's artifacts: a single way to access artifacts of all types.

Making Your Business Case

[A.3.3] So, why are we putting all of this focus on understanding how change requests fit into your existing process, and the various integrations available to you? Because you need to have a clear picture of where all of this fits into your organization if you're going to make a case for adding ClearQuest to the mix. If your management team is technically savvy, it might not be sufficient to present the team with the standard marketing materials available from IBM Rational's sales team. You'll probably need to roll out the full-frontal attack with white papers, technical specifications, or maybe even a visit from your local IBM technical sales team. However, for most companies, you're likely to just need a formal business case, outlining the benefits and the return on investment to your organization. For that, you'll need to dig into the details and to understand the potential impact of touching each and every one of the various tools and systems used by your development and product teams.

To sell management on ClearQuest, you need a strong business case. The business case is clear: Without the tools in place to translate customer feedback into requirements, requirement priorities into design specifications from product development, and implementation guidelines into finished code by engineering, and then to provide an update for the end user, your company's communication with your customers and with various internal teams can be chaotic.

The business driver behind ClearQuest is about helping your team decipher the communications between each intervener. That's the gist of what we're talking about when we discuss ClearQuest process and tool integration: How can we improve the customer service experience?

We can improve it by bolstering the feedback loops between engagement and development. We can improve it by expanding the communication between requirements and change management. We can improve it by helping management make better decisions on what functionality to build and when.

With all of these business benefits, integrating ClearQuest with the rest of the Rational Suite makes sense.

developerWorks Links

A.3.1   http://www-128.ibm.com/developerworks/rational/library/5535.html

S.3.1   http://www-128.ibm.com/developerworks/rational/library/4345.html

A.3.2   http://www-128.ibm.com/developerworks/rational/library/05/0816_ONeill/

A.3.3   http://www-128.ibm.com/developerworks/rational/library/content/RationalEdge/oct04/barnes/

4

Moving Parts

What kind of consumer are you? Are you the kind who buys a new product off the shelf, takes it home, carefully unpacks the product and accessories, and then begins to meticulously read through the instructions or user manual? No, of course not. That's a rare person, one who should be watched closely and not trusted with sharp objects.

Most of us react to the purchase of a new product much the way a four-year-old reacts to a freshly wrapped present on Christmas morning: We tear right into it. And so you may find yourself sitting on top of a newly installed defect-tracking system, proud of your team's accomplishment, but still a bit foggy on how the thing actually works. So, let's walk through some of the basics of ClearQuest navigation.

By no means is this chapter a comprehensive list of all the features and functions and doodads included in your ClearQuest release; rather, this is just a quick overview of the major activities you'll need to know to move around the inside of the application.

ClearQuest is a customizable defect- and change-tracking system, designed for working within a dynamic environment that requires steady workflows but also offers the ability to change on the fly. However, using the application itself is not *too* complicated. ClearQuest can manage every kind of change activity associated with software development—even with the base install.

As you grow familiar with its capabilities, you can begin to customize the application and realize its full potential. It shortens development lifecycles by unifying your entire team around a single process for defects, enhancements, and artifact modifications, as shown in the following examples.

- Development engineers can identify and prioritize action items that deal with their sections of the code.

- Test engineers can track the status and resolution of change requests to verify software quality.

- Project managers can get an overview of the effort, allowing them to better allocate development resources, streamline workflow, and accurately determine release dates.

- Administrators can integrate with ClearCase or another existing tool and customize it to fit the organizational needs.

For a complete and comprehensive overview of how to use ClearQuest, you're going to need to break the plastic seal on your user manual and commit yourself to some in-depth (and viscerally stimulating) reading. Or you can trap your team's ClearQuest administrator in the hallway and grill him or her for answers to all of your problems (most of which should probably relate to ClearQuest).

For the four-year-olds at heart, grab a bar of chocolate and settle down to read this chapter. At least it will provide you with the basics, and then you can move on to more complex topics at your leisure.

ClearQuest Fundamentals

[T.4.1] As you've probably already discovered, ClearQuest includes multiple interfaces into your data repository, for streamlined and consistent submission of change requests and easy access to the data within the underlying databases. With any standard installation, your system will include a complete change request lifecycle solution, which will allow your team to get up and running quickly. Right out of the box, ClearQuest allows you to immediately begin tracking your critical activities, such as assignment of tasks, prioritization of enhancements, and the all-important allocation of your limited resources.

[A.4.1] For those of you with a more robust set of applications in your change management ecosystem, ClearQuest also provides integration with those critical applications and management systems, such as ClearCase and Unified Change Management (UCM). Whether you are accessing ClearQuest from Windows, UNIX, or the web client, the basic capabilities remain the same: Users can submit change requests, view and modify existing records, and create and run queries.

Digging a little deeper into the mechanics, ClearQuest uses a three-tier architecture, as shown in Figure 4–1.

The first tier includes the various ClearQuest clients. Of course, for the web component, you will need to use a supported web browser. For the e-mail client, your administrator will need to configure the environment to allow ClearQuest requests through your e-mail server. To allow the ClearQuest e-mail reader to pull information into the systems, you'll also need to set up a dedicated e-mail account for ClearQuest. (ClearQuest supports Apache/Rational Web Server.)

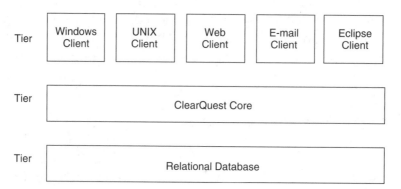

Figure 4–1   *ClearQuest architecture*

The second tier includes the core ClearQuest functions, including application logic and business rules. These APIs implement your specified business rules and regulate all access to the ClearQuest database.

The third tier is a relational database where ClearQuest stores change requests and metadata, such as user tables.

Future chapters provide more information on how to link existing systems to ClearQuest and how to further integrate ClearQuest within your change management ecosystem.

Change Request Lifecycle

One important concept to understand, before we dig deeper into the system, is that of the change request lifecycle. The first step in understanding this concept is to know the difference between an action and a state. An *action* is a step you take to resolve a request (open, close, assign, postpone, reject, validate, or duplicate). A *state* is a definition of where the change request is within the lifecycle (opened, closed, assigned, postponed, rejected, resolved, submitted, or duplicated).

Actions and states represent all of the various lifecycle variables your change requests can encounter within your process.

The standard ClearQuest training materials contain a great model, shown in Figure 4–2, that outlines each step of a basic software defect.

Let's introduce some additional terminology that you may find important as you navigate through ClearQuest.

In a relational database, you're probably familiar with the use of tables to organize your data. In ClearQuest, these tables are called *record types*. For example, *defects* and *enhancements* are two record types. There are two different kinds of record types: *state-based* and *stateless*. State-based records have a state transition model to represent their lifecycles in the defect- and change-tracking process; a stateless record type does not have these transitions. Once a user submits a new record of a stateless record type, it will stay in the database forever until it is explicitly removed. In other words, the stateless record type is suitable for records that do not require lifecycle tracking. The relationship between different record types is known as *referencing*.

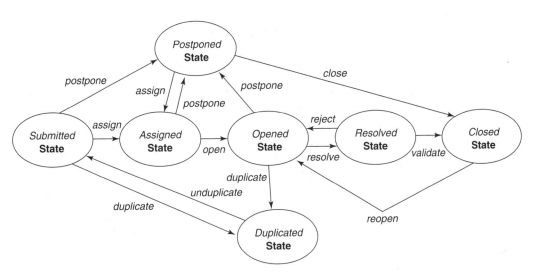

Figure 4–2   *Life of a software defect*

ClearQuest Components

As outlined in the ClearQuest manuals (see *Introducing Rational ClearQuest*, IBM Rational Software), ClearQuest consists of several components that work in a client-server environment. Table 4–1 describes these components.

Table 4–1   *ClearQuest Components*

Component	Used By	Use To
Client Tools		
ClearQuest for Windows	Everyone	Submit, modify, and track change requests; analyze project progress by creating and updating queries, charts, and reports
ClearQuest for UNIX	Everyone	Submit, modify, and track change requests; support project analysis by creating and updating queries
ClearQuest Web	Everyone	Access ClearQuest across multiple platforms using Netscape Navigator or Microsoft's Internet Explorer to submit, modify, and track change requests; support project analysis by creating and updating queries and reports
Administrator Tools		
ClearQuest Designer	ClearQuest administrator	Customize ClearQuest; manage ClearQuest schemas and databases; administer users and user groups
ClearQuest Import Tool	ClearQuest administrator	Import data, including records, history, and attachments from other change request systems and between ClearQuest databases
ClearQuest Export Tool	ClearQuest administrator	Export ClearQuest data from one ClearQuest user database to another user database
ClearQuest Maintenance Tool	Everyone	Set up and connect to the schema repository during installation and when upgrading to a new ClearQuest version
Rational E-Mail Reader	ClearQuest administrator	Enable ClearQuest users to submit and modify records by e-mail

ClearQuest includes predefined schemas that provide ready-to-use change- and defect-tracking processes, as well as standard integrations with various IBM Rational software products. You can use ClearQuest schemas out of the box or customize them to fit into your organization's workflow depending on your specific requirements.

ClearQuest provides the following support for your software development environment:

- Supports Microsoft Access, Sybase SQL Anywhere, Microsoft SQL Server, Oracle relational databases, and IBM DB2

- Integrates with IBM Rational ClearCase and Microsoft Visual SourceSafe so you can associate change requests directly with changes in your evolving software

- Integrates with Rational TeamTest, VisualTest, and the products now bundled as Rational PurifyPlus (Purify, PureCoverage, and Quantify), allowing you to submit change requests to ClearQuest directly from these testing tools.

- Works with Business Objects' Crystal Reports so you can create custom reports from ClearQuest data

- Allows you to integrate with other standard Windows tools, such as Microsoft Excel and Word, through an advanced Common Object Model (COM) interface

- Provides access to the Rational Unified Process (RUP) through the ClearQuest extended help menu

- Supports integration with all tools in the Rational Team Unifying Platform (TUP)[1]

- Provides seamless integration of ClearQuest into the Eclipse environment, through the ClearQuest client for Eclipse[2]

---

1. For more information about TUP, see http://www-306.ibm.com/software/awdtools/team/.

2. For more information about the ClearQuest Client for Eclipse, see http://www-128.ibm.com/developerworks/rational/library/04/r-3089/.

For more ClearQuest user questions, all the information you will need can be found in the ClearQuest online help on the IBM Rational website. Administrators, however, will want to track down copies of the following: *ClearQuest Release Notes, Installing Rational Clear-Quest, Administering Rational ClearQuest, ClearQuest Designer Tutorial,* the online help for ClearQuest Designer, and the *ClearQuest API Reference.*

Installation

We will offer just a couple of quick thoughts on installation. An important part of the installation process is the creation and configuration of the user databases for your implementation. Once added, the names of these databases then appear in the dropdown list of databases when users log in to ClearQuest. As the administrator, you will use ClearQuest Designer to set up user login accounts and to define user access privileges.

Moving Around in ClearQuest

[T.4.2] The first step is to log into the application, for which you must have a ClearQuest user account. When you reach the login screen, you must then select a database from the dropdown list. You'll have access only to those databases to which you are a subscriber. The administrator will control which databases you'll have access to and also help resolve any problems with your user account.

The ClearQuest main window appears once you open the application (Figure 4–3).

The Public Queries folder in the Workspace contains all of the standard ClearQuest queries, charts, and reports, as well as any custom items created by your administrator. The beauty of ClearQuest for the common user is that you can drag and drop any query, chart, or

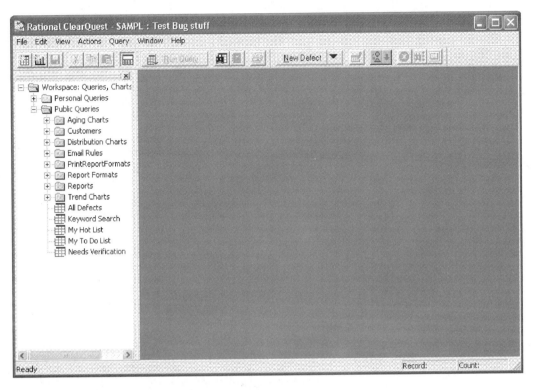

Figure 4–3   *ClearQuest main window*

report from the Public Queries folder over to your Personal Queries folder, and from there modify it to suit your own individual requirements. More about that in a minute.

Submitting Your Change Requests

The first action you might take in ClearQuest is to submit a change request. This creates a record in the user database that everyone on the team can view and track within the system. Within the Submit Defect form (Figure 4–4), you will describe the change request in detail and then attach any relevant code fragments and other supporting information that will help define the problem or suggestion and help the development team reach a quick and appropriate solution.

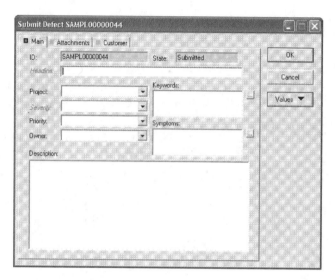

Figure 4–4   *Submit Defect form*

[S.4.1] Users can save frequently used field values as defaults so they won't have to reenter them each time they submit a change request. In addition, users can submit change requests directly into Clear-Quest from Rational TeamTest, Purify, PureCoverage, Quantify, and VisualTest. Or, they can submit and modify change requests by e-mail. It all depends on your existing or planned development processes—the system is fairly flexible.

When you submit a new change request, you will be prompted to select a record type. If you know the record type of your change request (e.g., you know it's a defect, or maybe it's a new product enhancement coming from someone on the product management team), then make the appropriate selection. If you're not sure how to define your request off the top of your head, just click the arrow and choose from the defined record types within the database you're accessing.

By this point, you've probably noticed that ClearQuest uses forms for data entry and display. The Submit Defect form is your primary window for submitting change requests; the slightly less intuitive Record form is where you'll review your change request records. In general, the Record form includes more information than does the Submit Defect form because the Record form is where all of the entered information is posted and summarized, whereas the Submit Defect form is a simple input screen. Take heart, however; your administrator can designate one of the forms to be both the Submit Defect form and the Record form, which will simplify the process by making one form represent both. So, no worries.

[S.4.2] Attachments are an important part of helping a user or customer describe an issue or enhancement. In fact, when dealing with external customers, the attachments (screenshots, documentation, and so forth) can be the one factor that helps development resolve an issue. ClearQuest allows you to attach any file to a record—that's right, it supports any format. Your attachments are stored directly in the database, and you can attach as many as needed. (All attachments can be seen as icons on the Attachments window within the Submit Defect form.)

One other important feature: Although it's not required, you can add keywords and symptoms to help define your change request. You can also select them from a dynamic pick list. Adding keywords and symptoms will help you search for your request and related records later when creating reports or searching for patterns in your change requests.

The ClearQuest administrator can also create additional record types. For example, you might want to separate different record types, such as hardware defects from software defects and enhancement requests. Again, the application is flexible enough to allow you to set up your processes to suit your needs. You can also customize Record forms, including adding tabs and fields and defining associated behaviors.

One concern with any change management system is whether or not people will log in and use it. A great automation feature, and one that helps alleviate this concern, is the ability for your administrator to configure ClearQuest to automatically send e-mail to various team members when a change request is submitted or changed. To take advantage of automatic e-mail notification, all ClearQuest users must set up their e-mail options.

Moving Change Requests Through the Workflow

You work with change request records by moving them through various states. In each state, you can perform actions such as modifying a record or moving it to another state. The Actions menu lists the actions that you can perform on the record while it is in any given state, including assigning, modifying, and opening and resolving change requests.

Your ClearQuest administrator can restrict actions to specific user groups. For example, the administrator might allow everyone on a team to resolve a change request, but restrict the verify action to members of the quality assurance group.

Tracking Your Change Requests

ClearQuest queries make it easy for everyone on your team to track change request records as they move through your system. This is done primarily through *personal queries* and *public queries*.

Any queries, charts, and reports created by a user are stored in that user's Personal Queries folder. (See the next section for a discussion of charts and reports.) The ClearQuest Query Wizard will walk you through the process of building a custom query. It will prompt you on the fields you want to display, as well as all of the fields and corresponding values you want to use as query filters. To modify an existing query, first drag the query to your Personal Queries folder and then use the Edit Filter and Edit Display Field Wizards. (See Editing an Existing Query in Chapter 9, page 163.)

Certain ClearQuest packages also include ready-to-use queries that help you locate records by project or component, by assigned engineer, by level of severity, and so on. The ClearQuest Administrator can save queries to the Public Queries folder and can assign this privilege to other users. ClearQuest users with admin access can copy any of their personal queries into the Public Queries folder to make those queries available to anyone with access to the appropriate user database.

Gathering Project Metrics

[S.4.3, S.4.4] A change management solution is only as good as the data it generates to let you manage your development processes. Certain ClearQuest packages provide predefined charts and reports that you can run on Windows and on ClearQuest Web to view the status of your project at a glance. You can also create your own customized reports and charts.

ClearQuest charts display record data graphically. Distribution charts show the current status of data; trend and aging charts show historical information. ClearQuest also includes reports and report formats that you can use to create reports from ClearQuest data. You can also use Crystal Reports Professional Edition to create new report formats. You can save these formats in your Personal Queries folder and use them to format ClearQuest reports. Remember that the ClearQuest online help contains detailed information to assist you every step of the way.

Obviously, this section does not cover all of the capabilities of a standard ClearQuest installation. We're just attempting to jump-start the process and show you how easy it is to navigate through the basic features of ClearQuest. Please check your user manual if you have more specific questions.

Administering and Customizing ClearQuest

For complete information about administering ClearQuest, including a description of how to get your users up and running, see *Administering IBM Rational ClearQuest*, which you should have received with your software. (You can also pull the manual from the IBM website.) Either way, you've got a lot of reading to do. The following subsections provide a summary of the tasks ahead of you.

ClearQuest Databases and Schemas

[A.4.2] Now we're starting to get into the nuts and bolts of your change management system. A ClearQuest *schema* contains the metadata that defines the process for how users work with records in ClearQuest. The schema includes the following:

- Record type definitions

- Forms used to submit and modify a record

- Field definitions and behavior

- States a record can be in

- Actions used to modify or change the state of a record

- Hooks written in VBScript or Perl that further customize fields and actions

ClearQuest includes several predefined schemas that you can use as provided or customize to fit your workflow; you can also create and implement your own schemas. What you do depends on your development processes and your comfort level with the system. If you're relatively new to the system, your best bet is to implement the standard ClearQuest configuration out of the box and then slowly modify the system as your users and administrator grow more comfortable with the system.

ClearQuest stores schemas in a *schema repository*. A ClearQuest installation usually consists of one schema repository and one or more user databases, depending on how you segment your user population. You can have separate user databases for each project or group several projects together in one database. Something important to consider, however, is that if you want to generate reports and charts across *several* projects, you will want to put the projects in the same database.

Another important note: Projects that share a database *must* use the same schema; once a database is associated with a schema, it can be upgraded only with a newer version of that same schema. In other words, the database cannot use an older version of the schema or a completely different schema—so plan accordingly.

Starting ClearQuest Designer

A ClearQuest schema defines the process of working with a record, along with the Record form and relevant fields. Records have a variety of different states. The defect record begins in the Submitted state; from there you can change the state of the record to Closed, or you can modify the record without changing its state. However, to further automate your system, the administrator will use ClearQuest Designer to make targeted changes to the overall schema. Again, you can start with the standard schema and make changes after everyone feels more comfortable with the application.

At this point, you will want to do some customizations. Here are some of the steps and activities.

1. *Check out the schema*. To customize a schema, you must first check it out of the schema repository.

2. *Add a new state*. The ClearQuest Designer State Transition Matrix shows the various states that a record can be in and the actions that move the record from one state to another.

3. *Add a new action.* The Actions grid shows all of the actions that can be performed on a record. To add a new action, you first add the action to the Actions grid and then associate it with the appropriate states.

4. *Create a new field.* To create a new field, open the Fields grid. This grid shows all of the fields on the Record form, their types, and their default values.

5. *Define the behavior of the new field.* The Behaviors grid shows how fields behave when the associated record is in each state. You can define whether a field is read-only, mandatory, or optional in each state, or define default behavior for all states. You can also create a user behavior that restricts user access to the field. Open the Behaviors grid, then right-click on the field and use the popup menu to define the behavior of the field.

6. *Add a new field to the Record form.* After creating a field, you must add it to the Record form.

7. *Create an action hook.* A *hook* is a trigger for pieces of code that ClearQuest executes at specified times to more fully implement your workflow. ClearQuest provides many predefined hooks that you can easily modify to suit your needs. You can also use the ClearQuest API to write hook code in Microsoft VBScript or Perl.

   ClearQuest supports four types of hook code.

   - *Field hooks* provide a way to validate the contents of a field or to assign field values.

   - *Action hooks* implement tasks at key points in the lifecycle of a record.

   - *Record scripts* allow you to associate a hook with a control, such as a pushbutton or a shortcut menu option, on a single record.

   - *Global scripts* allow you to reuse hook code within other hooks.

Use the ClearQuest Script Editor to edit the hook so that it initializes the value of the associated field.

8. *Check in the schema.* At any time while working on a schema, you can test your work in progress. This upgrades the test database with your latest changes, which provides a quick way to test your changes in the ClearQuest client without affecting your production user database.

   When you're satisfied that your schema changes are working correctly, check the schema into the schema repository. Once the schema is checked in, you can use it to upgrade your user database. ClearQuest prompts you to back up the schema repository and the database before upgrading.

9. *Select a ClearQuest schema.* Table 4–2 shows a list of the predefined schemas included in ClearQuest (see *Introducing*

Table 4–2   *Predefined Schemas*

Schema	Description
AnalystStudio	Is compatible with Rational Suite AnalystStudio. Contains customization for use with Rational RequisitePro.
Blank	Contains only system fields. Use this schema to create a schema from scratch.
Common	Contains metadata that is common to all of the ClearQuest schemas.
DefectTracking	Contains the fields necessary to start using ClearQuest to track defects in a software development environment.
DevelopmentStudio	Is compatible with Rational Suite DevelopmentStudio. Contains fields and rules that work with Rational Purify, Quantify, and PureCoverage.
Enterprise	Is used with Rational Suite EnterpriseStudio. Contains fields and hooks that work with all Rational products.
TestStudio	Is compatible with Rational Suite TestStudio. Contains fields and rules that work with Rational TeamTest, RequisitePro, Purify, Quantify, and PureCoverage.
UnifiedChangeManagement	Supports the UCM process by providing integration with Rational ClearCase.

Rational ClearQuest). ClearQuest schemas consist of various packages that provide specific functionality. You can add individual packages to an existing ClearQuest schema or to your own customized schema. For a full list of schemas and descriptions, see *Administering Rational ClearQuest.*

Coming Up for Air

You should now have a basic understanding of how to navigate your way through the application and perform some of the more important administration functions. Obviously we've taken great liberties to remove all of the specific information about how to accomplish your tasks and replaced them with general information and pretty pictures. We're hoping that you get the gist of it and are ready to move forward. Feeling confident? For detailed information on what we've just covered, please review the ClearQuest Designer help index. Otherwise, let's now move on to some more complex topics.

developerWorks Links

T.4.1	http://www-128.ibm.com/developerworks/rational/library/4194.html
A.4.1	http://www-128.ibm.com/developerworks/rational/library/2111.html
T.4.2	http://www-128.ibm.com/developerworks/rational/library/4194.html
S.4.1	http://www-128.ibm.com/developerworks/rational/library/4513.html
S.4.2	http://www-128.ibm.com/developerworks/rational/library/3883.html
S.4.3	http://www-128.ibm.com/developerworks/rational/library/3936.html
S.4.4	http://www-128.ibm.com/developerworks/rational/library/4327.html
A.4.2	http://www-128.ibm.com/developerworks/rational/library/4114.html

5

Analyzing Your Company's Needs

Ah, the smell of newly opened packing material in the morning. You just received a rather large shipment from the front desk, and now sitting on your desk is an unwrapped set of disks and manuals with "ClearQuest" written all over them. Where do you start? How do you design a successful ClearQuest deployment? Well, the best place to start is by outlining the problem domain and then reaching an understanding of all the pieces to the puzzle. Think of it as a holistic approach to problem solving: Before attempting to solve any kind of problem, it's always good to map out all of the artifacts in the system, define the relationships among the artifacts, and figure out the best solution with the broadest perspective.

Without question, the time and effort spent in up-front planning saves time and effort down the road. Adequate time and resources should always be made available for planning your project.

Actors

[A.5.1] Before understanding *how* to use ClearQuest, you first need to understand *who* will be using the application. It's always best to do a bit of planning before moving forward with an implementation, so let's start with a use case analysis of your development system. When defining the components of your system, where is the best place to start? You should always start with the actors.

Actors are the ClearQuest users or relevant systems (the "who" or the "what") that will use—or be used by—ClearQuest.

If you come from a very process-oriented organization, just had a lot of time on your hands, and have already started with your own development system analysis, good—you're ahead of the game. Basically, draw a circle around your ClearQuest actor and pull whatever use cases you have already created from your analysis.

If you're starting from scratch, the first step is to list each user type that will be accessing your new ClearQuest system. Table 5–1 provides some examples of common actors you might encounter, with each of their primary responsibilities.

Obviously, this list is not exhaustive. Your organization may also involve several roles within the product management organization, or you may want to include field representatives. The key here is to write down everything you can at this time; in other words, document as much as you understand about the current system and all the actors that may need access to the system. Don't worry about trying to determine what each of these actors will be doing in the system (submitting, reviewing, and so on). It's easier to remove actors once you have all the components defined. Later in the process, you will determine which actors interact with ClearQuest and which ones don't, so it's better to err on the side of too much information now rather than trying to add an actor later.

Table 5–1 *Human Actors*

Actor	Description
Administrator	The ClearQuest administrator keeps everything up and running. The administrator usually makes changes to the design, database schema, and implementation.
Customer	This is the customer of the product that your team will be developing (i.e., the end user). The customer may need reports from ClearQuest or direct access to the enhancements or defects that he or she has reported.
Change control board (CCB)	Change control boards are commonly used to monitor and track the changes being managed for the upcoming product release.
Developer	The software developer is responsible for making changes to the software as it relates to enhancements or defects.
Tester	The tester will (hopefully) find all of the defects and report them before the product goes out the door. Testers are responsible for validating any changes to the product in the released builds of the product.
Tech writer	The tech writer is responsible for changing the documentation to describe new enhancements to the product or to correct errors found in the documentation.
Manager	The manager is responsible for making the team more productive. The manager typically assigns change requests to individual developers, tech writers, or testers.
Business analyst	The analyst may work with the product or engineering teams to help define internal processes or could be an external customer liaison in solution definition and development who needs access to the system.

Humans are not the only actors that interact with ClearQuest. The software that will integrate with ClearQuest is just as important to document as the human actors. Table 5–2 provides examples of software that could be part of a development system with ClearQuest.

Figure 5–1 shows the typical set of actors associated with ClearQuest.

Table 5–2   *Software Actors*

Actor	Description
Microsoft Project	Microsoft Project keeps track of the projects; it can be integrated with ClearQuest to show the amount of time spent on individual tasks to fix a defect or enhancement. This gives the manager a better mechanism for predicting completion of the product.
ClearCase	The version control system should be tied to the changes made in the system; in other words, it should correlate to defects and enhancements.
RequisitePro	RequisitePro keeps track of requirements. Some of these requirements turn into enhancements for the product.
Legacy bug system	The current defect-tracking system contains information that will need to be put into ClearQuest.
Remedy (CRM system)	Customer support typically has another system to keep track of calls and also the changes that need to be made to the product.

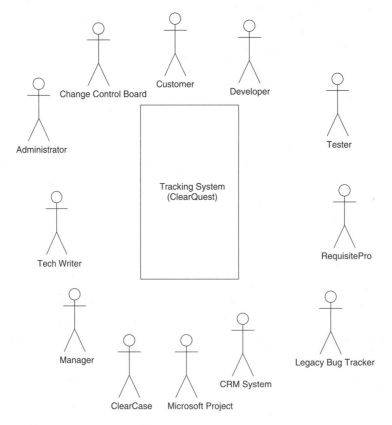

Figure 5–1   *ClearQuest actors*

Use Cases

A *use case* is a sequence of actions that an actor performs within a system—in this case, ClearQuest—to achieve a particular goal. A good use case should describe one aspect of the system without presuming any specific design or implementation. In other words, a use case describes *what* the system needs to do without specifying *how* the system will perform.

Here's an example of good use case text:

> The data entry clerk types his or her user ID and password and then submits this information to the system. The system ensures that the user ID is valid and that the password matches the stored user ID, and then. . . .

And here's an example of bad use case text:

> The data entry clerk types his or her user ID and password and then presses the OK button (located in the lower right-hand corner of the window). The system goes out to the SystemUser table and uses the entered user ID as the key into the table. . . .

The text of a use case describes possible paths through the use case. This text includes the actions that the actor performs and the system's responses to those actions. These paths are captured as *flows of events*.

Two kinds of flows of events are associated with use cases.

1. The *main flow of events* (sometimes referred to as the *basic course of action*) is the sunny-day scenario, the main start-to-finish path that the actor and the system will follow under normal circumstances. The assumption is that the primary actor doesn't make any mistakes, and the system generates no errors. A use case always has a main flow of events.

2. An *exceptional flow of events* (or *alternate course of action*) is a path through a use case that represents an error condition or a path that the actor and the system take less frequently. A use case often has at least one exceptional flow of events; in

fact, the more interesting behavior described by use cases is often found in the alternate courses.

The basic idea is this: Each use case should address one or more requirements in text that's easy to understand quickly for everyone involved in the project, whether technically savvy or not.

Use cases provide very important benefits to your planning efforts. For one, they help you visualize the problem space and the relationships of the various actors. For another, they help you identify any missing actors. They also force you to think about the various steps in your existing process and whether those steps will meet your needs when ClearQuest has been fully implemented—or whether you're going to need to make some changes.

Taking the actors described earlier, we can quickly find some use cases that each actor can perform with respect to the implementation of ClearQuest. Figure 5–2 illustrates some examples of the use cases found in a standard ClearQuest implementation.

Your use cases should include some descriptive text or scenarios that show how each actor interacts with the system. Here are some examples.

- *Create Defect*: The customer or tester creates a defect by defining a title of the defect, a description, the severity of the defect, the type of defect, the product version, the product build, and the date by which the defect should be resolved.

- *Create Enhancement*: The customer creates an enhancement request for the product. He or she specifies a title for the enhancement, a description, the criticality of the enhancement, the version of the product he or she is using, and the date by which he or she would like to have the enhancement.

- *Assign Change Request*: A change request is created when a developer or tech writer is assigned to perform work toward

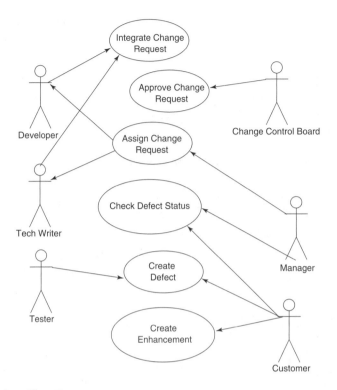

Figure 5–2   *ClearQuest use cases*

an enhancement or a defect. The manager assigns the change request.

- *Approve Change Request*: When the developer or tech writer makes a change to the product, he or she will advise the change control board that the change is ready for review before it gets integrated into the system.

- *Integrate Change Request*: The developer or tech writer integrates the change request into the product using ClearCase UCM once the change control board has approved the change for integration.

This should make sense whether or not you are well versed in the Unified Modeling Language (UML) and use case analysis. If you follow these steps, we promise that you'll have a better understanding of your current systems and users and how best to deploy Clear-Quest.

You can also use this information to develop the workflows, which will help you determine just how you will need to customize Clear-Quest to fit your needs.

Activity Diagrams

An *activity diagram* is a variation on the traditional flowchart. In the context of ClearQuest, we'll use activity diagrams to illustrate work-flows between use cases.

On an activity diagram, a use case is represented by a sort of lozenge shape—a symbol with long, straight lines on top and bottom and short sides that are curved outward (see Figure 5–3). Other features of activity diagrams include branching and merging, as well as forking and joining.

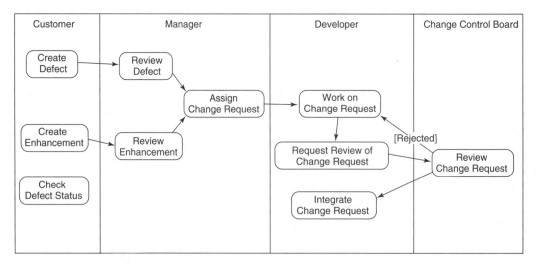

Figure 5–3   *ClearQuest activities*

- A *branch* is a decision point at which there are two or more possible paths of flow of control. A *merge* is a point at which two branched paths come together. Both branches and merges appear as diamonds, just as branches do on flowcharts.

- A *fork* is a splitting of a flow of control into two or more flows of control, each of which operates independent of and concurrent with the others. A *join* is a synchronization of two or more flows of control into one flow. Both forks and joins are represented as long, thin, black rectangles called *synchronization bars*.

An activity diagram can also show *swimlanes*. Each pair of these lines, which are generally vertical, delineates one group of activities or use cases. These are very useful for showing which part of an organization or which specific actors are involved in which use cases within your workflow.

You should begin mapping your workflows by examining the use cases you specified earlier. Include an activity for each use case, and add a swimlane for each actor using the given use case.

Next, draw the typical flow of activities among the use cases. In most cases, you will find that you need to add *more* activities than you have use cases. Again, don't worry about the amount of content at this stage—it's all part of the refinement process.

In Figure 5–3, we've added a few additional activities to help round out a typical flow of activities and to help you understand how to approach your model.

Now that our high-level use case workflow or activity diagram is complete, we can look at more detailed activity diagrams. You should continue to elaborate (a fancy word that means *to refine* or *to build upon*) the workflow until you have enough information that you can show the end users of the system—and those folks who will be actually designing and deploying the system—just what the system will be doing. This is where the "art" of deployment comes into play: With too little finessing, you could end up developing something the users don't want, whereas too much creativity in your planning process could waste your own time. Don't fall victim to analysis paralysis. The key is to elaborate *just enough*.

This is rather vague, we know, but there is no definitive stopping point. At some time, you need to draw the line and move forward with your implementation.

One important elaboration involves starting to find the objects involved in the workflow so that you can easily change the workflow, adding data objects and their proposed states to the high-level activity diagram. An *object flow* is simply a dependency that shows the details of how the object(s) involved in the various activities or use cases on the diagram are specifically affected.

In Figure 5–4, we add three objects, along with the state each object is in, during the workflow. Remember, this is still a very high-level depiction.

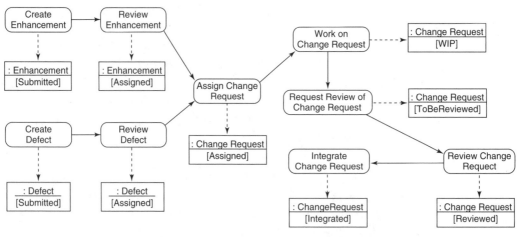

Figure 5–4   *ClearQuest workflow*

Reports

[A.5.2] What's the use of implementing a new application or system if you can't generate reports for management? OK, you may also have some use for pulling metrics out of ClearQuest—it wouldn't be unheard of. Let's face it: People like to look at lists.

The key here is to talk to the actors that will be using the system and ask them the following questions.

- What types of reports will the users need?
- What do the reports look like?
- What kind of information is important for the users?
- Does the information need to be in detailed or summarized form?
- When will the users need to see this information?
- Can the users use a website to see the information, or do they need the application installed?
- How often will the users see the report?

Still not convinced that you need reports out of your system? Well, someone somewhere may eventually ask you for a report, so you might as well be prepared. Common reports that people use in defect/enhancement-tracking systems include the following:

- *Open change requests assigned to me*: Shows the user what work he or she needs to do for a given day, week, or month
- *Open defects or enhancements for a specific version of the product*: Shows what defects or enhancements need to be resolved for a version of the product; typically used by the manager to see the progress of work
- *Defects or enhancements that need review*: Typically used by a change control board to see what changes need to be reviewed for approval or rejection

- *Defects or enhancements that have been integrated into a product*: Typically used to see how much work has been accomplished for a given version of the product

- *Defects or enhancements submitted by a customer*: Typically used by customers to find out when a defect or enhancement will be resolved and available in the product

- *Trends of defects*: Shows open and close rates per version, for example (not the only trend that can be reported); typically used by management to determine progress on a product

Ask a user what kinds of reports he or she would like to see, and you're going to open up a huge can of worms. The list can be very long, so try to focus on those reports that are used daily first, then weekly, and then periodically. The daily and weekly reports should be considered when designing your system, while the more periodic reports can be pushed out. ClearQuest is fairly flexible, and any missing reports or standard queries can always be added later. However, you should ask the questions, understand the requirements, and make sure the information for *all* of your reporting requirements are in the database in the first place.

Again, don't go overboard on examining all of the report possibilities available to your company. Don't get stuck in analysis paralysis. Find out which requirements are necessary and which are nice to have, and plan accordingly. Don't worry: The topic of reports will pop up again when we elaborate the design.

developerWorks Links

A.5.1   http://www-128.ibm.com/developerworks/rational/library/04/r-3091/

A.5.2   http://www-128.ibm.com/developerworks/rational/library/398.html

6

Designing Your System

[T.6.1] After you have determined your organization's needs, the next step in your analysis is to find the classes of objects described in your use cases and workflow.

One of the best places to begin looking for classes is to examine the nouns in your use case descriptions. Look for nouns and noun phrases such as *change request, product, title, version, build,* and *product.* It sounds too simple, we know. Once you have all of your nouns, you then need to classify them into as few classes as you can. Finally, you will throw out any classes that will not be useful for the implementation.

For those of you new to this process, don't worry—we're about to provide some explanations of how your classes are constructed and how they fit into your overall system design.

Classes

What is a class, anyway? Well, a *class* is a collection of objects that have the same characteristics, including structure and behavior. An object that belongs to a particular class is often referred to as an *instance* of that class. One might think of a class as an abstraction of a particular group of real-world things or concepts and an object as the concrete manifestation of that abstraction. (Within the Clear-Quest database, classes map to record types.)

Class Notation

The standard UML notation for a class is a box with three compartments, as shown in Figure 6–1. For more information about the UML in general, we recommend reading *UML Distilled Second Edition* by Martin Fowler with Kendall Scott, *Unified Modeling Language User Guide, Second Edition* by Grady Booch, James Rumbaugh, and Ivar Jacobson, or *Visual Modeling with Rational Rose 2002 and UML* by Terry Quatrani.

The top compartment contains the name of the class. The middle compartment contains the attributes—in other words, the data values—of the class. The bottom compartment contains the class's operations—the functions that the class can perform.

You can show a class without its attributes or its operations; the name of the class can appear by itself. Later in this chapter, we'll show some example classes whose operations compartments have been suppressed.

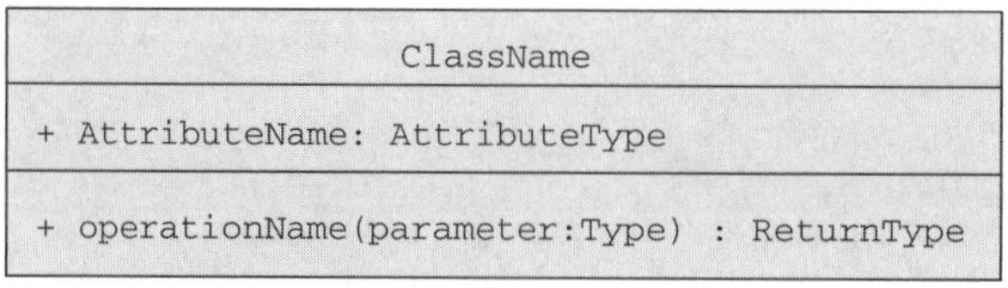

```
                        ClassName

+ AttributeName: AttributeType

+ operationName(parameter:Type)  : ReturnType
```

Figure 6–1   *UML class notation*

Class Relationships

Classes, by themselves, aren't particularly useful. Instead, the relationships among classes provide the foundation for the structure of a new system.

The most common type of relationship among classes is the *association*. This is a simple structural connection among two or more classes; an association between a pair of classes is by far the most common form.

An association is represented by a straight line between the classes, as shown in Figure 6–2.

This example also provides information about the multiplicity of the association. A *multiplicity* value indicates how many objects that belong to each class can be present within the association. In the example, Class A has a relationship that involves zero or more objects belonging to Class B. (You can use the ReferenceList attribute within ClearQuest Designer to map this kind of design element to your implementation.)

Finding Classes

The first step in designing the structure of your ClearQuest system involves finding the classes of objects described within your use cases and workflows, which we addressed in Chapter 5. Look for the nouns in your use case descriptions. Once you have all of your nouns, make decisions as to which nouns should be classes and which nouns should represent attributes on those classes. These are the prime guiding principles: If a noun has interesting characteristics, it's a good candidate to be a class. If a noun is really more of a

Figure 6–2   *UML association notation*

description of a characteristic of something else, it's a good candidate to be an attribute.

Some Class Examples

Let's combine these simple graphical elements to form a working example for a defect-tracking system, as shown in Figure 6–3.

There are four classes in this example: Defect, Enhancement, Customer, and Change Request. Attributes are defined for each class, and we've also defined some relationships. Notice that the Enhancement class has two relationships with the Customer class, one named "primary" and the other unnamed. This allows an Enhancement object to have a primary Customer object and also a list of other

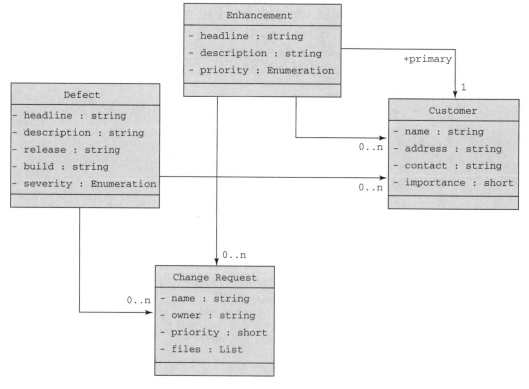

Figure 6–3   *Defect-tracking system classes*

Customer objects that require the Enhancement object. Additionally, Enhancement and Defect objects have zero to many associated Change Request objects; this arrangement allows for multiple changes against the same defect or enhancement.

Statechart Diagrams

Knowing the possible states in which your objects can reside is important with regard to your ClearQuest implementation, as ClearQuest allows for direct mapping from state nets to implementation. You should coordinate your state nets with your workflows so you can implement how changes in state affect other objects in your system.

States and Transitions

A *state* is a condition in which an object can be at some point during its lifetime, for some finite amount of time.

An object can do any or all of the following while it's in a particular state:

- Perform some activity
- Wait for some event
- Satisfy one or more conditions

Figure 6–4 shows the notations for a regular state and for two special kinds of states: the *start state*, which represents the initial conditions in effect when the object is created, and the *end state*, which represents the conditions in effect when the object is terminated.

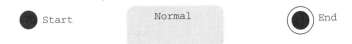

Figure 6–4   *UML state notation*

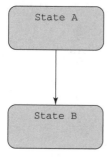

Figure 6–5   *UML transition notation*

A *transition* is a change of an object from one state to another. A transition "fires" when an event of interest to the given object occurs. A directed line between the "from" state to the "to" state represents a transition, as shown in Figure 6–5.

A transition may have a label on it that shows the action that "triggers" the transition. It can also have a *guard*, which is a Boolean expression that must evaluate to True before the transition can fire. Adding this kind of information to transitions usually proves highly useful in making design decisions.

States and transitions appear on *statechart diagrams*. Figure 6–6 illustrates the lifecycle of a typical change request.

Charts and Transitions

ClearQuest has a mechanism to view the same state and transition information in a matrix. While the matrix form can show only part of the information that a statechart diagram can show, it's easier to see what is going on.

Table 6–1 illustrates an additional way to show the same state net represented within Figure 6–6.

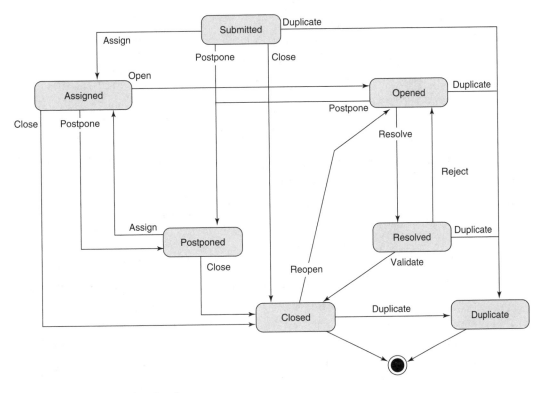

Figure 6-6   *Lifecycle of a change request*

Table 6-1   *ClearQuest Transitions in Table Form*

To/From	Submitted	Assigned	Opened	Resolved	Closed	Duplicate	Postponed
Submitted							
Assigned	Assign						Assign
Opened		Open		Reject	Reopen		
Resolved			Resolve				
Closed	Close	Close		Validate			Close
Duplicate	Duplicate		Duplicate	Duplicate	Duplicate		
Postponed	Postpone	Postpone	Postpone				

User Interface Design

You need to know when and how your users will work with the classes that you specified in your design. Where do you find this information? Look at your use cases. Specifically, look closely at any use cases that involve a human actor. If you have a human actor interacting with an object of a specific class, you will need to design a user interface form for that class. In fact, you may need to supply more than one interface.

Let's look at our use cases and see what we can find.

System-Level Design and Deployment Diagrams

To understand how you are going to deploy the tool, you need to have some concept of who is going to use it and where. For example, does it need to be accessed remotely? Do you need Windows or UNIX support? Do you need both? If so, you need to understand all of the available deployment options.

To understand the different deployment options, you first must understand how ClearQuest is architected. As we showed at a high level in Chapter 4, ClearQuest uses a three-tier architecture. Table 6–2 takes this a step further, showing each of the deployment options for each tier.

The Client layer of the ClearQuest architecture includes a variety of modules and tools for entering and viewing data, creating and managing schema and databases, importing and exporting data from other environments, and replicating data across multiple locations. It also includes the ClearQuest API.

The Business Flow layer, or the ClearQuest core, is the layer where application logic and business rules are stored and executed. The ClearQuest core communicates with the database layer using Open Database Connectivity (ODBC) drivers. The ClearQuest core also

Table 6–2   *ClearQuest Tier Deployment Options*

Layer	Components
Client layer	ClearQuest client (both Windows and UNIX)
	ClearQuest Web (both)
	ClearQuest Designer (Windows)
	ClearQuest Maintenance Tool (Windows)
	ClearQuest Import Tool (Windows)
	ClearQuest Export Tool (Windows)
	ClearQuest User Administration (Windows)
	ClearQuest API (both)
	ClearQuest MultiSite (both)
	ClearQuest Eclipse plug-in (both)
	Command Utilities (both)
	Rational E-Mail Reader (Windows)
Business Flow layer	ClearQuest core
Database layer	Microsoft Access
	SQL Anywhere
	Microsoft SQL Server
	Oracle RDBMS
	IBM DB2
	ODBC drivers

exposes a limited amount of core functionality through the Clear-Quest API for hook-scripting purposes.

The Database layer contains the database management system or systems that physically manage the information in the schemas and user databases.

In the Windows environment, the database management system can be any of the following:

- Microsoft Access (small installations, fewer than five users)
- SQL Anywhere (small or medium-sized installations)
- Microsoft SQL Server, Oracle RDBMS, or IBM DB2 (large installations)

You need the correct Windows software to design and maintain your ClearQuest installation. Unfortunately, because the UNIX version does not contain the designer or maintenance tools, you must install the Windows version of the toolkit. If you can avoid using ClearQuest on UNIX and just have a Windows installation, your life will be much easier.

There are also options for your users to use the web interface on UNIX and Windows with a pure Windows version. The only reasons to stick with UNIX on any of the layers, in our view, would be as follows:

- Client layer: Users need to use the API, or ClearQuest itself, natively on a UNIX platform. If your users want to use the native tool but do not have a requirement to use the API, then offer them ClearQuest Web.
- Database layer: If you have a very large installation, you might want to use a UNIX box over a Windows box.

If you can avoid a UNIX installation of any sort, you will be better off. The simple fact is that it is always more difficult to manage multiplatform deployments than a single platform. So stick with Windows if at all possible.

developerWorks Links

| T.6.1 | http://www-128.ibm.com/developerworks/rational/library/4201.html |

7

Implementation: Schema and Database Design

[A.7.1] No amount of contingency planning can prepare you for every possible problem. At some point, though, you need to cross that thin line between discussion and action to officially begin your implementation.

At this stage, you've outlined all of the actors and use cases, you understand your user and management expectations, and you have made some fundamental decisions about how to set up ClearQuest. Now it is time to start defining your database.

There are several options available with regard to the type of database to use with ClearQuest. Looking at your deployment design, which we addressed in previous chapters, helps in the decision. Of course, if you are using a Windows platform, you will have different options than if you are using a UNIX platform. You may also have your hands tied with using a specific database, depending on business or licensing agreements. Some organizations have corporate agreements with database vendors, so make yourself familiar with all of your system and software restrictions before committing yourself to any development efforts.

This is yet another example of why it is important to understand your entire system design before moving forward. A decision to change your database may also change your system design.

ClearQuest supports the following types of databases:

- Microsoft Access
- SQL Server
- SQL Anywhere
- Oracle
- DB2

We address specifics associated with each of these later in this chapter.

Picking a Schema

Table 7–1 describes the various schemas that are built into ClearQuest.

[S.7.1] One approach to deciding which schema will work best for you involves starting with the Blank schema and adding the things you want as you become more accustomed to the tool and as your users understand how the tool fits into the way they work. This is an acceptable way to go, but you could end up wasting a lot of time—don't forget that you'll also be responsible for implementing the solution, debugging, and so forth. Another choice might be to select

Table 7-1   *ClearQuest Schemas*

Schema	Description	Best Used For
Blank	Contains only record types Used to create a schema from scratch	Best used for custom projects that you set up from the start
Common	Contains fields and record types common to all predefined schemas Included in each ClearQuest schema (which consists of this schema and one or more packages)	A generalized solution when multiple teams will be using ClearQuest and you will expand over time
DefectTracking	Contains the fields necessary to start using ClearQuest to track defects in a software development environment	Field and test teams
AnalystStudio	For use with Rational AnalystStudio Contains fields and rules that work with Rational Rose and RequisitePro	Architects, designers, and prototype implementations
DevelopmentStudio	For use with Rational DevelopmentStudio Contains fields and rules that work with Rational PurifyPlus	Developers, QA, and CM teams
TestStudio	For use with Rational TestStudio Contains fields and rules that work with Rational TeamTest, RequisitePro, Purify, Quantify, and PureCoverage	A more specialized solution for test teams using these other IBM Rational products
Enterprise	For use with Rational EnterpriseStudio Contains fields and hooks that work with most Rational Suite products Enabled for UCM	End-to-end development using Rational tools such as ClearCase, PurifyPlus, Rose, and RequisitePro
UnifiedChange Management	Provides support for integration with UCM and sets up ClearQuest to use the predefined ClearCase policies	Integration with ClearCase UCM

the Enterprise schema, which has everything but the kitchen sink (and don't be surprised if the next version of ClearQuest includes that, as well). Again, going with this option could be a waste of time. However, with the Enterprise schema you could be wasting not just your time but also the time of your engineers, managers, and others who would need to provide input, test the solution, and ultimately might not have their needs met by this implementation.

So, what should you do?

Your goal should be simplicity: Pick the schema that offers the minimum features you need, and then add to your solution over time. By taking this approach, you'll find that you can implement much faster and get your customers working quickly and with more productivity.

Using ClearQuest Designer

[T.7.1] If you are using ClearQuest for the first time, you will need to create a database schema and databases. You do this with the Clear-Quest Designer tool, which you find in the Start menu: Rational Software → ClearQuest → ClearQuest Designer. You will first need to log in, using the window shown in Figure 7–1.

By default, the user is "admin" and there is no password.

Once you have logged in, ClearQuest will automatically present you with a schema to open. You can select an existing schema, or you can simply close this window.

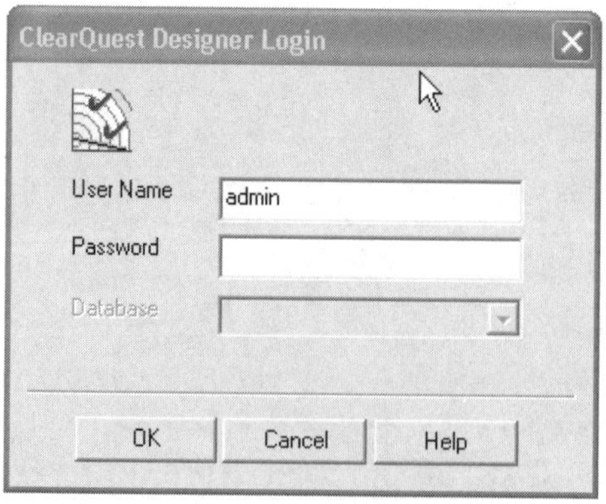

Figure 7–1   *ClearQuest Designer Login window*

Working with Users and Roles

[A.7.2, A.7.3] There are two major approaches to working with users in your ClearQuest design: Let everyone have access to everything, or restrict users or groups of users to specific actions and data within the database. This is where the size of your organization, your security requirements, and the level of control you need play an important role in your efforts regarding user and role assignment.

In the first case, the solution is very easy: You don't worry about any users or groups and just tell everyone the admin password. Then they can log on to ClearQuest as the admin user and basically do whatever they want. This is typically not very reasonable, though, so you probably won't choose this option.

[S.7.2, S.7.3] A variation of this approach creates a few user accounts that allow for specific types of access to the application. This option requires some planning. First, you have to look at all of the actors of your system; you could easily create a user for each human actor you have. Then you give the password to everyone who fits the role from the use case analysis, as we described in Chapter 5.

The downside of this approach, as you will quickly learn, is that you have no real audit trail on who did what. Additionally, the passwords for the different users are shared, and people will quickly find the user who has the most privileges and use that user ID all of the time. The upside of using this model is that you have to add only a small number of users, and you typically have to do it only once, so no real user management is required.

[S.7.4, S.7.5] Worth mentioning is that version 2003.06.15 of ClearQuest (and anything newer) offers support for the Lightweight Directory Access Protocol (LDAP). For many enterprise customers, this is a great option for user management.

You can easily add a user with the User Administration tool, which you can access from the Windows Start menu or the ClearQuest menu option Tools → User Administration. The window shown in Figure 7–2 appears when you open this tool.

To add a user, select User Action → Add User, as shown in Figure 7–3.

This brings up a dialog box you use to fill in the relevant information for each user you need to add to ClearQuest (Figure 7–4). As you can

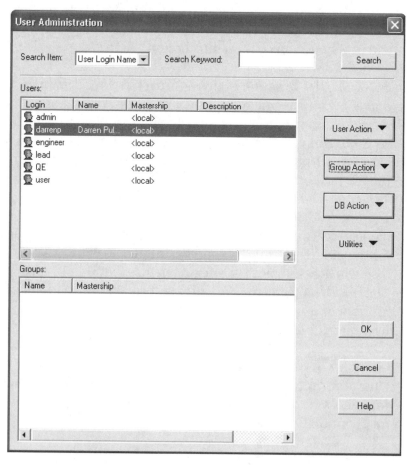

Figure 7–2   *User Administration window*

Figure 7–3   *Adding a user*

see, this is time consuming: It can take each of several people several days for a large organization.

The last option we'll discuss, which is the one that offers the most control—and, unfortunately, calls for the most work—involves adding all of the users that will be using ClearQuest to specific

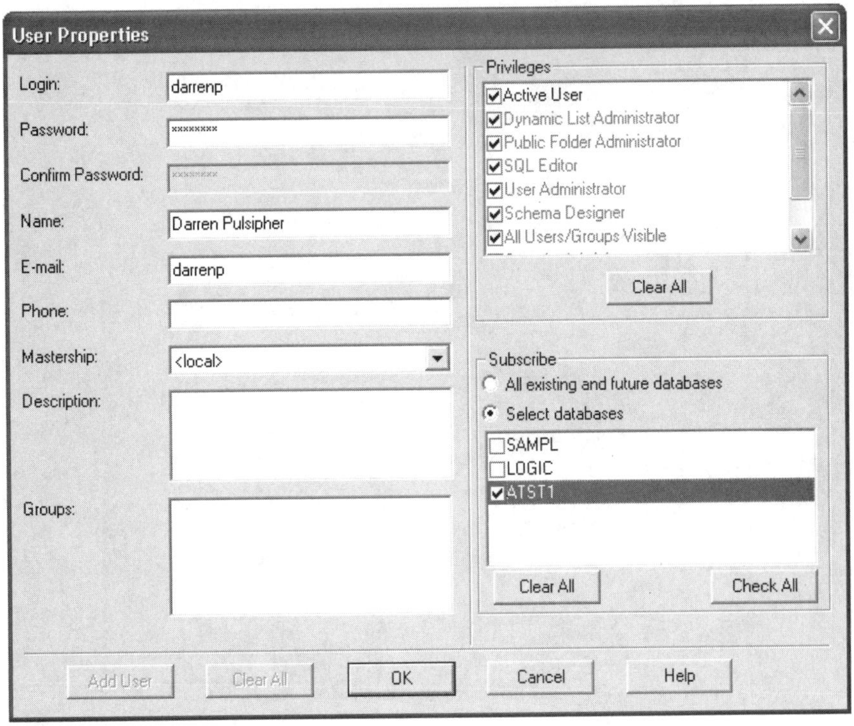

Figure 7–4   *User Properties window*

groups that match the actors from the results of your use case analysis. Since it is very time consuming to do this all by hand, using ClearQuest's API is a good option to consider.

[S.7.6] Before writing the script to automatically create all of the users, start by creating all of the groups. To create a group, select User Action → Add Group. The dialog box shown in Figure 7–5 will appear.

The name of each group should match that of an actor from your use case model. If you have already added users, you can add the users to each group you create. When you are done, click OK.

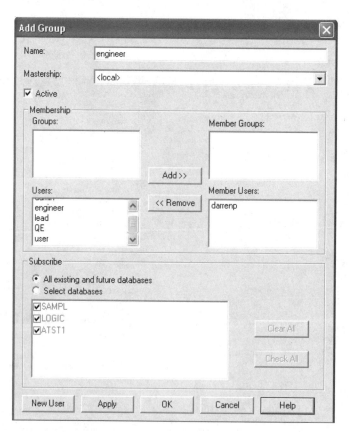

Figure 7–5   *Add Group window*

Now that you have all of your actors represented by groups in the system, you can write a script that will add all of the users from your Windows active directory to ClearQuest. There are several script examples available on the IBM Rational website. Peter Vogel provides a script designed to synchronize the ClearQuest user database with NT users at http://www-128.ibm.com/developerworks/rational/library/3934.html/.

Working with Existing Schemas

If you choose to work with a schema from the default selector, you have to choose one. See the earlier section about the different schemas for information on how to select the best schema for you.

Before clicking Finish in the Open Schema window, make sure you choose a schema to check out or view, as shown in Figure 7–6. If you actually want to work on changing the schema, you will need to check it out. (Don't worry about the mechanics of ClearCase checkouts; ClearQuest has its own little version control system.)

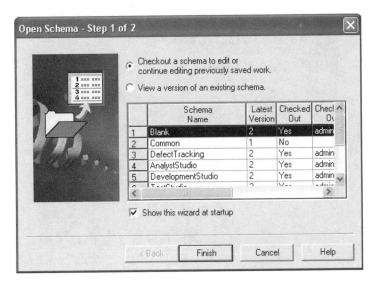

Figure 7–6   *Selecting a schema*

If you want to open and work with another schema, you can use the File → Open Schema menu option.

Creating New Schemas and Databases

If you want to create a new schema, select the File → New Schema menu option (Figure 7–7).

ClearQuest will present a list of schemas on which you can base your new schema (Figure 7–8).

Once you have chosen a schema, ClearQuest prompts you to name your schema and also to provide a comment (Figure 7–9). Make sure that your schema has a descriptive name (e.g., not JoesTest or MyProduction).

After you have named your schema, ClearQuest will ask if you want to associate a database with the schema (Figure 7–10). This is typically a good idea. It will first ask for a logical database name and a comment.

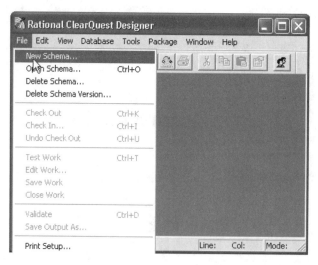

Figure 7–7   *Creating a schema*

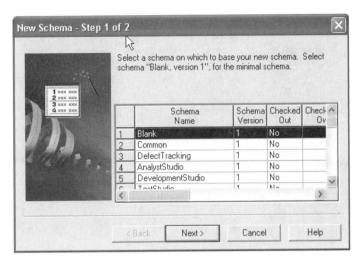

Figure 7–8   *Schema list*

Database names can be between one and five characters in length. The first character of the name must be a letter (uppercase or lower-case).

Next, you need to decide what type of database software you will be using and select it in the dropdown Vendor menu (Figure 7–11).

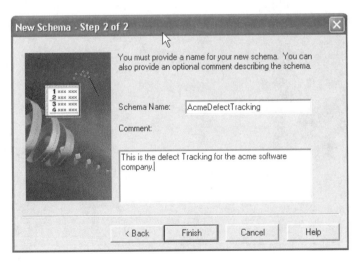

Figure 7–9   *Naming a schema*

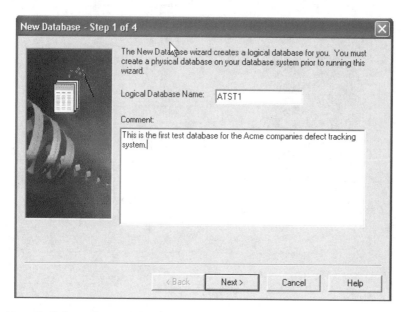

Figure 7–10   *Defining a logical database name*

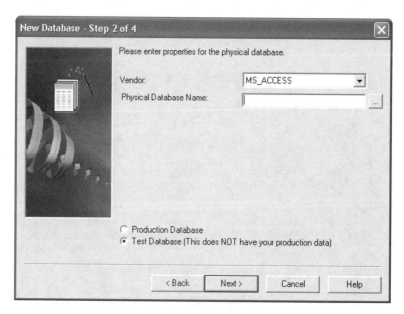

Figure 7–11   *Defining database properties for a new schema*

Earlier in the chapter, we discussed the different options and which tool would be best to use. Note that this step involves selecting the vendor, entering the name of the database, and indicating whether the database is a production or test database. (Starting with a test database first will allow you to test your database before moving it into production.)

[A.7.4] The next step has to do with responsiveness and use of licenses. If you set the polling interval to too small a value, it can result in decreased performance. Additionally, if you change the timeout variable to a number lower than the default, as shown in Figure 7–12, you can share licenses more easily, but you could block someone from using the tool if he or she were idle for even a short period of time.

[S.7.7] The last step is to select the schema with which to associate the database (Figure 7–13). This should be the schema you just created.

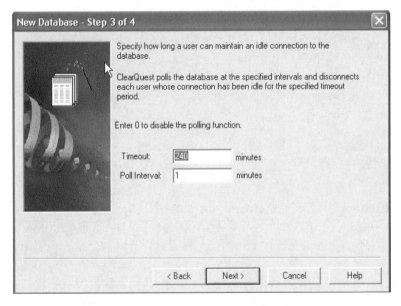

Figure 7–12   *Defining user idle time*

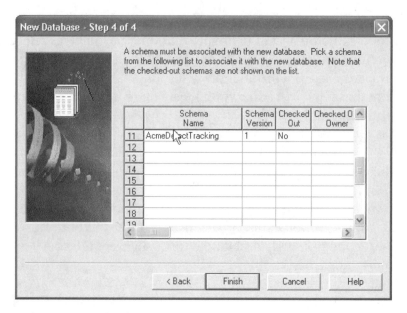

Figure 7–13   *Associating the database with the schema*

Setting Up Database Options

The previous section describes the steps involved in creating a database. The next step in working with a new database involves different options depending on the type of database you select. The following subsections address how to set up the options specific to each type of database.

Microsoft Access

First off: If you are going to use the ClearQuest Web interface or ClearQuest MultiSite, you cannot use Microsoft Access. Access is useful for playing around with data exported from ClearQuest but is not recommended for enterprise data or particularly critical data.

If you do want to use Access, you need to make sure that you have a shared unified naming convention (UNC) path available on which to put your database, such as \\CQMaster\databases, as shown in

Figure 7–14. (UNC is a Windows path-naming convention.) If not, then you will basically be creating a database that can be used only on the machine you're working on.

In the Physical Database Name box, you need to enter the name for the schema repository and the full path to the schema repository file using a UNC-style path (e.g., `\\DevServer\ProjectShare\CQ_DBS\` `schema_repo.mdb`).

You can browse to the directory containing the database. Be sure to browse using Network Neighborhood to preserve the UNC-style path name. When is this useful? When you're first starting to prototype your schemas and your databases, this is perfectly fine to use. Just remember that you will probably need to create production databases using one of the other options.

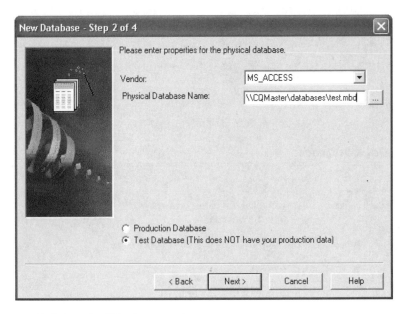

Figure 7–14   *Defining the Windows path*

SQL Server

SQL Server is the most likely candidate if you are using Windows-only solutions. This option requires setup on the SQL Server side, as well as the ClearQuest (client) side.

Let's first look at the ClearQuest side. You will need to add values in several fields. Table 7–2 describes the fields, which are shown in Figure 7–15.

The next step is to enter the database name for the SQL Server schema repository and then enter the name of the database server. One thing to remember: Each ClearQuest native client must be able to access this server host name exactly as it appears in this entry, so be case sensitive, and make sure your naming conventions adhere to any native client restrictions.

Next, enter the database owner user name (e.g., dbo or Administrator) in the Administrator Name box. Then enter the password for the database owner and add the general-purpose user name, followed by the password for the general-purpose user name.

Table 7–2 *Database Fields*

Field Name	Field Purpose	Example
Physical Database Name	The physical database name for the schema database	Schemas
Database Server Name	The database server name, by which all ClearQuest clients must be able to access this host	ClearQuestProduction
Administrator Name	The name of the owner of the database	dbo
Administrator Password	The password of the owner of the database	
Connect Options	Any additional SQL Server connection options	

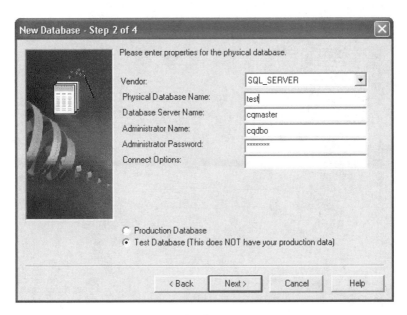

Figure 7–15 *Defining database properties for SQL Server*

Finally, enter the schema repository or read-only user name in the Read-Only User Name box, and then the password for the schema repository or read-only user name.

SQL Anywhere

Another database option is SQL Anywhere (Figure 7–16). The process of setting the database options is much the same for SQL Anywhere as for Microsoft Access. In the Physical Database Name box, enter the name for the schema repository and the full path to the schema repository file using a UNC-style path (e.g., \\DevServer\ProjectShare\ CQ_DBS\schema_repo.mdb).

You can browse to the directory containing the database by using Network Neighborhood, which preserves the UNC-style path name.

Enter the properties for the physical database as follows: First, add the name of the database server; then, select the protocols used to communicate with the SQL Anywhere server. Enter the database

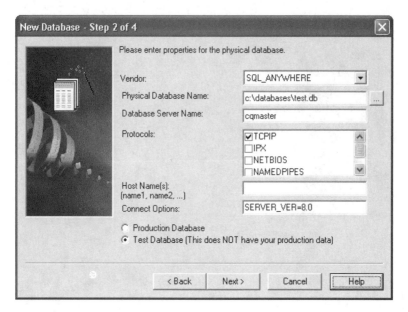

Figure 7–16 *Selecting database options for SQL Anywhere*

host name in the Host Name(s) box. (Host Name(s) is a required field.) For TCP/IP, this can also be the IP address. Alternatively, if you are using TCP/IP as your network protocol, you can specify the IP address of the physical database server in the Host Name(s) box. Please note that the database host machine *must* be visible to the client machines using network share and using one or more of the communication protocols.

Next, enter the version of SQL Anywhere that you are using in the Connect Options box. For SQL Anywhere 5.0, enter SERVER_VER= 5.0. For SQL Anywhere 8.0, enter SERVER_VER=8.0. If you leave the field blank, the ClearQuest Maintenance Tool will default to SQL Anywhere 5.0.

Oracle

Still another option is Oracle. Add the Oracle user name you created for the schema repository, and then enter the password for the user name in the Password box (Figure 7–17).

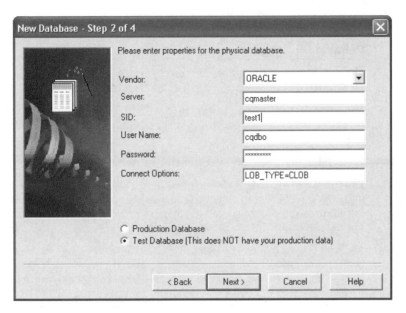

Figure 7–17   *Selecting database options for Oracle*

As shown in the ClearQuest Designer's Guide, the following options (described in Table 7–3) need to be typed in the Connect Options box, separated by semicolons. For example:

```
Host=name; SID=name; Server_ver=8.1; Client_ver=8.1;
Lob_type=LONG or CLOB
```

Remember that all ClearQuest users must use the same alias or net service name (TNS name), database instance (system ID or SID), TCP/IP protocol, and host name (Oracle server host).

NOTE: From ClearQuest version 2003.06.13 onward, you no longer need the Oracle client to be installed, and you don't need the TNS alias. ClearQuest now uses Data Direct drivers to connect to Oracle databases.

Table 7–3   *Oracle Connect Options*

Option	Definition
HOST	The name of the database server host. (If your ClearQuest environment includes UNIX and Windows clients, this name is mandatory.)
SID	The name of the database instance. (If your ClearQuest environment includes UNIX and Windows clients, this name is mandatory.) On UNIX, the SID is case-sensitive.
SERVER_VER	The version of the Oracle server you are using. (For Oracle 8i, use 8.1.)
CLIENT_VER	The version of the Oracle client software you are using. (For Oracle 8i, use 8.1.) If ClearQuest client users want to use a different Oracle client version than what the administrator enters here, they'll need to override the set options manually. The default setting is 8.1.
LOB_TYPE	The type of data you will be using. The valid data types are either LONG or CLOB. If your existing databases default to LONG, do not change them to CLOB. Databases already implemented with the LONG LOB_TYPE property are incompatible with CLOB. However, there are limitations using the CLOB data type. For more information on restrictions and guidelines, consult the *Release Notes* for ClearQuest.

DB2

[A.7.5] Your final option is to use IBM's DB2. Enter the database alias name (the name of the alias pointing to the DB2 database) for the schema repository in the Database Alias box, then add the DB2 user name created for the schema repository. Finally, enter the password for the user name (Figure 7–18).

Worth noting is that with DB2, ClearQuest can point to a single, physical database server—as long as each ClearQuest database uses a unique login name. You do not have to create an alias for each DB2 client.

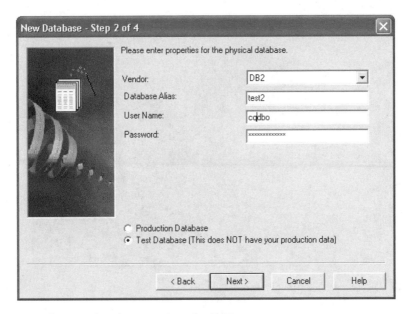

Figure 7–18   *Selecting database options for DB2*

Scripts (Basic or Perl)

[A.7.6, A.7.7] Once you've created a schema, you can start changing aspects of it. First, select Schema Properties in the browser window on the left, as shown in Figure 7–19.

[S.7.8] You really have only two options, BASIC or Perl, to use as your scripting language for Windows. Here we will show our bias toward consistency. If you're working with a cross-platform implementation, we suggest using Perl for Windows as well as UNIX. It will make your life much easier. If you are just doing a Windows installation, and you don't know Perl, then use what you know. There's nothing worse than learning a new tool and a new language at the same time.

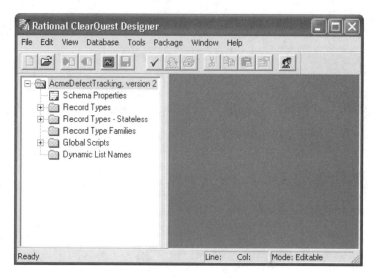

Figure 7–19   *Selecting Schema Properties*

developerWorks Links

A.7.1	http://www-128.ibm.com/developerworks/rational/library/4114.html
S.7.1	http://www-128.ibm.com/developerworks/rational/library/content/03July/2500/2834/ClearQuest/clearquest_plugins.html
T.7.1	http://www-128.ibm.com/developerworks/rational/library/4857.html
A.7.2	http://www-128.ibm.com/developerworks/rational/library/271.html
A.7.3	http://www-128.ibm.com/developerworks/rational/library/04/r-3091/
S.7.2	http://www-128.ibm.com/developerworks/rational/library/4333.html
S.7.3	http://www-128.ibm.com/developerworks/rational/library/3899.html
S.7.4	http://www-128.ibm.com/developerworks/rational/library/4351.html

S.7.5	http://www-128.ibm.com/developerworks/rational/library/4358.html
S.7.6	http://www-128.ibm.com/developerworks/rational/library/4516.html
A.7.4	http://www-128.ibm.com/developerworks/rational/library/05/1115_diebolt/
S.7.7	http://www-128.ibm.com/developerworks/rational/library/3895.html
A.7.5	http://www-128.ibm.com/developerworks/rational/library/04/r-3090/
A.7.6	http://www-128.ibm.com/developerworks/rational/library/4702.html
A.7.7	http://www-128.ibm.com/developerworks/rational/library/4711.html
S.7.8	http://www-128.ibm.com/developerworks/rational/library/3888.html

8

Implementation: Customizing the Schema and Creating Hooks

[A.8.1] As you start to get more comfortable with ClearQuest and begin to look for ways to customize, you'll need to have a deeper understanding of the different components that make up the schema.

Record Types

Records can be mapped directly to the classes you developed as a result of your analysis and design. Just remember that each record corresponds with a record in the database.

There are two basic record types: state-based and stateless. *State-based* records have associated state nets. *Stateless* records have no state, but they have additional information that is valuable to using the tool. Examples of stateless records include attachments, users, history, and integration records.

Record Type Families

To create a record type family that allows a ClearQuest user to run a single query across multiple record types, you can simply group two or more state-based record types that have common fields. However, there are two things to keep in mind.

1. Record type families must contain one or more common fields (fields that are the same in each record type). These common fields are the only ones that can be used to query the family.

2. Because record types and record type families appear in the same window when a ClearQuest user clicks Query → New Query, you should use a naming convention that helps users distinguish individual record types from record type families.

To create a record type family, you will first add a family and then create common fields. You can also remove members from a family and rename or remove the family.

Fields

Fields map to attributes and relationships in the class designs you generated when you worked on your system design. (If you haven't designed your system yet, winging it will make your experience with ClearQuest horrible.) Before we tell you how to add a new field, though, let's explore the characteristics of a field, as shown in Figure 8–1.

The characteristics, from left to right, are as follows.

- *Field Name*: This is the name of the field you are adding. This should be the same as the attribute name of the relationship role from your design.

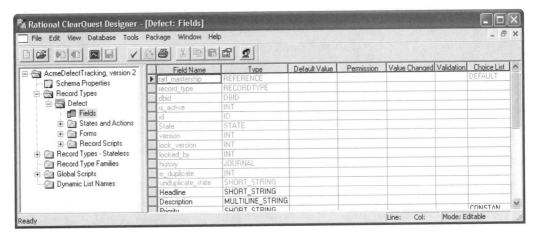

Figure 8–1   *Field characteristics*

- *Type*: This is the database type associated with the field. This does not map directly to the type of attribute in your design, but it comes pretty close. Table 8–1 shows the valid values defined in the ClearQuest Designer's Guide for this field and their uses.

- *Default Value*: This is the default value that ClearQuest will assign to this field when it creates the record. The options here are None, Constant, or Script; you can use the latter to specify a script that ClearQuest can call to create a default value on the fly. (The hook for the default value of the field is called at the beginning of a submit action.)

- *Permission*: You can select None, or you can specify a script to permit the user to change this field. If you write a script, it must return one of the `BehaviorType` constants that indicate the user's access to the field. Use this hook to force workflow and/or security. (See the online *API Reference for Rational ClearQuest* for enumerated constants.) If you add a permission hook to a field, you must modify the Behaviors grid so that at least one of the field's behaviors is set to `USE_HOOK`. Failure to do this will result in a validation error.

Table 8-1   *Type Values*

Data	Description/Comments
ATTACHMENT_LIST	A value that allows records to store files related to the record.
DATE_TIME	SQL date and time.
INT	A SQL integer.
MULTILINE_STRING	A variable-length string of unlimited size.
REFERENCE	A reference to a unique key in a record type. For REFERENCE type fields, you must select a state-based or stateless record type to refer to. You can also enter an optional back-reference field to create a link from the referenced record back to this field's record. Also, you can specify that the referenced record type is under security control.
REFERENCE_LIST	Multiple references to unique keys in record types. REFERENCE_LIST fields allow you to reference multiple records within a field. You can use REFERENCE_LIST fields with a parent/child control to link related records.
	For REFERENCE_LIST type fields, you must select a state-based or stateless record type to refer to. You can also enter an optional back-reference field to create a link from the referenced record back to this field's record.
SHORT_STRING	A variable-length character string with a 254-character maximum. You set the length in the Properties dialog box when defining the field. Enter a value between 1 and 254 in the Maximum Length field. When a user enters a value in a field of type SHORT_STRING, ClearQuest automatically trims any leading or trailing spaces.

- *Value Changed*: You can select None, or you can specify a script for ClearQuest to call when the value is changed. Use this hook to trigger updates for other fields. This can be used to modify dynamic lists or change system behavior. After running this hook, ClearQuest will validate any field that has changed as a result of running this script.

- *Validation*: ClearQuest will call the routine you specify here in order to validate the user's input before changing the value. You can specify None.

- *Choice List*: If you want the user to select from a list, you can change this value to a constant list or use the scripting language to generate a list.

Adding a Reference to Another Object as a Choice List

The following subsections describe various aspects of ClearQuest choice lists.

Adding a Reference to Another Object

Given a class design, you can easily create an object reference to implement a relationship with another object. There are two types of references: REFERENCE, which is for relationships whose cardinality is 0..1, and REFERENCE_LIST, for cardinality of 0..n.

For either type of field, you must provide information that specifies the record type to which the field refers. You can fill this in by using the property dialog for the field in the record (Figure 8–2) and then using the Reference To choice list to select the record type to reference.

The given field can refer to either a state-based or stateless record type. (Note that you need to create the record type before it will appear

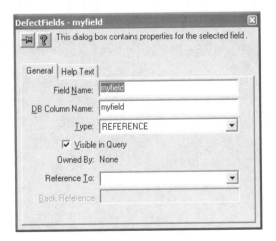

Figure 8–2   *Changing field properties*

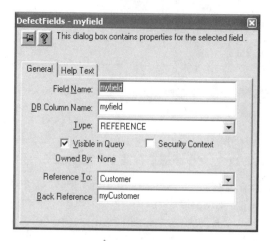

Figure 8–3   *Specifying a back-reference value*

in the choice list.) Typically, you'll want to create all of your records first and then come back to define your relationship-based fields.

If the relationship has the ability to navigate in both directions, you can specify a back-reference value (Figure 8–3).

ClearQuest will create a new field with the specified name (Figure 8–4).

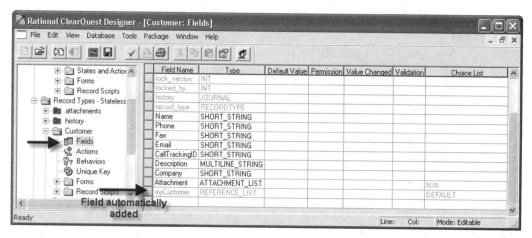

Figure 8–4   *Creating a new field*

Adding a Multiple-Choice List

Sometimes you want to restrict the user to multiple choices for a field value. You can do this by selecting the field and then selecting the type of choice list you wish to use. You have the following options.

- SCRIPTS allows users to write a BASIC or Perl script that returns a lists of choices.

- CONSTANT provides a set of values that don't change.

- DYNAMIC is convenient for lists that you want to change frequently because it enables you to update the list values without changing the schema. See the next section for information about how to do this.

- DEFAULT is useful for both REFERENCE and REFERENCE_LIST types.

Select NONE if you don't want the user to have a choice list.

Writing a List of Choices with a Script

You can also specify a script that will return a list of choices for the user. When you select a script, a dialog will appear and ask you to choose one of these options.

- [A.8.2] *Recalculate Choice*: ClearQuest will recalculate the list with the script each time the user asks to populate the field. A word of warning with regard to this option: This will cause the script to run *much* more often than you might think. Any time *any* field value changes, the choice lists for other fields will be recalculated if this option is checked. This is a major contributor to schema performance problems, so use this option carefully. Another option is to explicitly use the InvalidateChoiceList API call properly to force the ChoiceList script to run only when necessary.

- *Limit to List*: This option will limit the list to the values returned by the script; it does not allow the user to enter any other value.

[S.8.1, S.8.2] Your script can be written in BASIC or Perl. The following script is written in VBScript. Note that the name of the sub is the `<fieldName>_ChoiceList`, where `<fieldName>` is the name of the field for which the choice list script is written.

```
Sub fieldName_ChoiceList(fieldname, choices)
    ' fieldname As String
    ' choices As Object
    choices.AddItem("Blue")
    choices.AddItem("Red")
    choices.AddItem("Yellow")
    choices.AddItem("Green")
End Sub
```

The following is the Perl equivalent.

```
sub fieldName_ChoiceList {
    my($pFieldName) = @_;
    my @returnChoices;
    push @returnChoices, "Blue";
    push @returnChoices, "Red";
    push @returnChoices, "Yellow";
    push @returnChoices, "Green";
    return @returnChoices;
}
```

Adding Dynamic Lists of Choices

[A.8.3] Dynamic list field hooks are convenient for lists that you want to change frequently because they enable you to update the list values without changing the schema.

Before you can use a dynamic list choice for a field, you must first create a dynamic list in the database schema.

First, right-click on Dynamic List Names within your database schema workspace, and then select Add from the popup menu that appears (Figure 8–5).

Then type the name of the list in the new list item. Now you can use this dynamic list in connection with any field's choice list, as shown in Figure 8–6.

Simply go to the list for any field, and then select Dynamic List. A dialog box opens (Figure 8–7). Select which dynamic list you wish to use.

Now, you're probably asking yourself, "What about the values in the list?" You actually use a dynamic list in the ClearQuest client

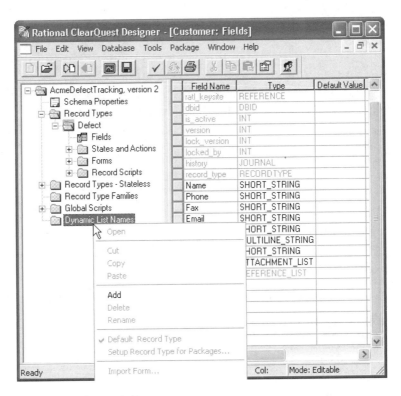

Figure 8–5   *Adding a dynamic list*

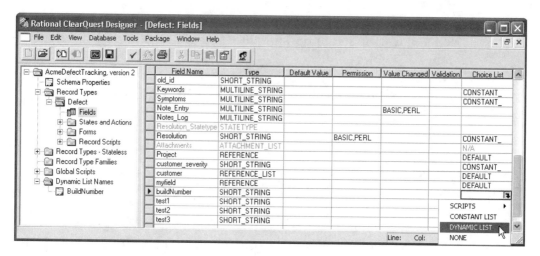

Figure 8–6   *Using a dynamic list*

application without changing the schema. Please note, though, that you must have schema designer, dynamic list administrator, or superuser privileges to edit a dynamic list. To change or add values to a dynamic list in the ClearQuest client, select Edit → Named Lists and select the list you want to edit.

States

[A.8.4] Before you begin working with states, make sure that you have state nets designed for each class in your design. Otherwise, specifying states within ClearQuest can quickly become a confusing exercise.

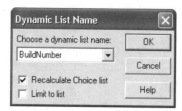

Figure 8–7   *Dynamic List Name window*

Adding a New State to a Record

Setting up states, actions, and transitions for your classes (records) is typically a two-step process: Add the states, and then add the transitions. Note that you shouldn't add a single state and then its transitions because the tool wasn't designed to work in this fashion, and you will quickly become frustrated. It's best to add all of the states first, then put in the transitions, and specify the actions last.

The first step is to open the record to which you want to add states, and then open States and Actions → State Transition Matrix (Figure 8–8).

To add a state, click on the empty box to the left-hand side of the spreadsheet, and then type a name for the state (Figure 8–9).

Go ahead and do this for each of the states in your state net.

Adding Transitions to a State

Now we're ready to add the transitions for each state. (ClearQuest Designer allows the addition of transitions only between states that already exist.)

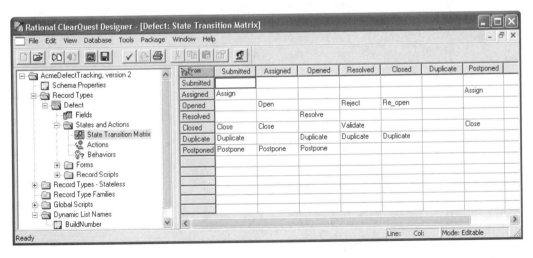

Figure 8–8 *State Transition Matrix item*

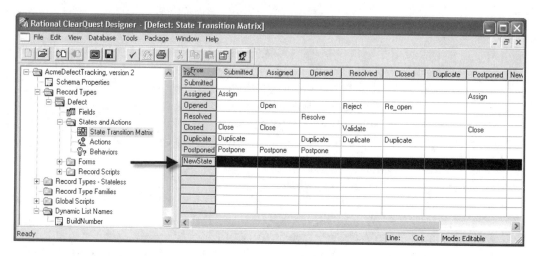

Figure 8–9   *Adding a state to the matrix*

To add a transition, go to the Actions item (Figure 8–10).

Now, right-click on the left column, or on the Actions item itself, and then select Add Action (Figure 8–11).

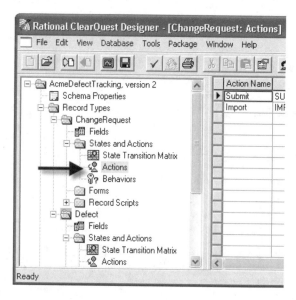

Figure 8–10   *Actions item*

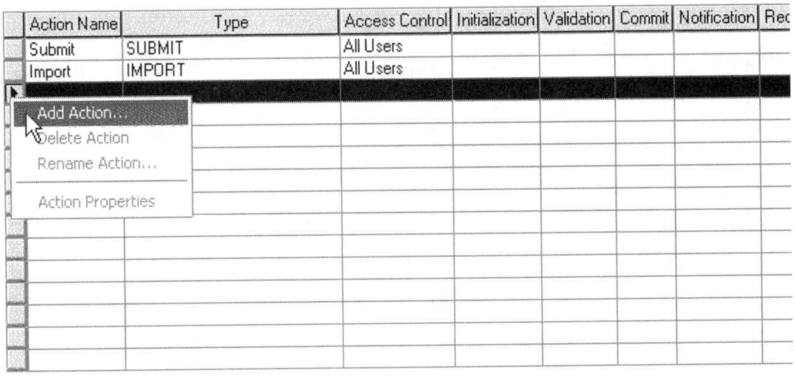

Action Name	Type	Access Control	Initialization	Validation	Commit	Notification	Rec
Submit	SUBMIT	All Users					
Import	IMPORT	All Users					

Add Action...
Delete Action
Rename Action...
Action Properties

Figure 8–11   *Selecting Add Action*

You will need to give your transition a name, which can come from your design. Figure 8–12 shows the dialog box.

If you have an unnamed transition, now is a good time to name it. This name should be a verb phrase. You also need to set the type to Change_state.

Now select the State tab. You should see a list of source states and destination states. Look in your design to see if there is more than one state that this transition can come from, and select all of the associated source states (Figure 8–13).

This is how you would map the given state net to the state source and destination values.

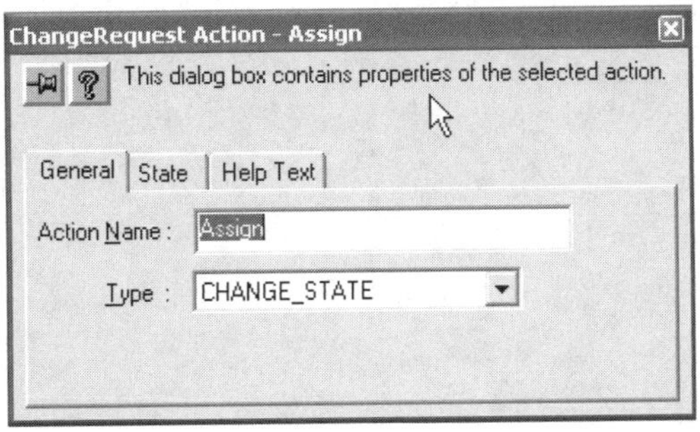

Figure 8–12   *Naming your transition*

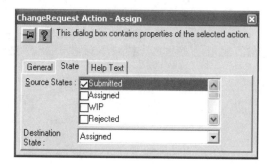

Figure 8–13   *Selecting a source state*

Now the transition should be defined. To check this, click on the State Transition Matrix icon; you should see your action show up as a transition between the given states, as shown in Figure 8–14.

You should be able to define the rest of your transitions the same way. When you're done, make sure that everything matches your state net diagrams.

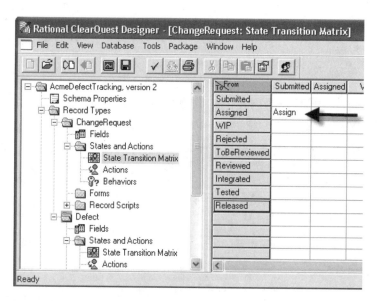

Figure 8–14   *Checking your transition*

Adding Actions to a State

Actions can be used for more than just transitions. For example, if an action is performed on a given record, that action doesn't change the record's state. Actions generally map to the operations on the classes within your design.

ClearQuest Designer allows for several different types of actions. The list in Table 8–2, which was taken directly from the ClearQuest Designer's Guide, shows the various types and what they can be used for.

Forms

Forms are a mechanism that allows the designer to create user interface elements. The number of forms per record and when they're available can be derived from the user interface design discussed in Chapter 6.

Adding New Forms for a Record

Open the record for which you want to add a form from the schema browser on the left side of the workspace editor. Select Forms, and then right-click and select Add (Figure 8–15).

The window shown in Figure 8–16 should appear.

ClearQuest provides a graphical user interface editor that you can use to add controls, fields for input or display, restrictive views, and tabs for categorizing information.

Specifying Permissions for Tabs and Forms

Before you start filling in your user interface design, go back and look at your use cases again. Specifically, determine which users have

Table 8–2 *Actions*

Action Type	Description/Comments
Base	A Base action is a secondary action that runs as a side effect of every other action. Base actions let you write an action hook only once, but use it with multiple actions. Each time an action fires, the Base action checks to see if the hook criterion is met; if it is, the base action completes its process. For example, you can add a Notification action hook to a Base action to have the Base action automatically send e-mail notification when a Close action (a Change_state action type that moves the record to the Closed state) occurs. Base actions do not appear in the list of actions in the Clear-Quest client.
Change_state	Change_state actions are available only for state-based record types. A Change_state action moves a record from a source state to a destination state. A Change_state action can reference many source states, but only one destination state. Change_state actions appear in the list of actions in the ClearQuest client only if the current record is one of the source states.
Delete	Delete lets users delete a record from the database. Delete actions appear in the list of actions in the ClearQuest client.
Duplicate	Duplicate is available only for state-based record types. A Duplicate action links the record to another record that contains similar information. Duplicate actions appear in the list of actions in the ClearQuest client only if the current record is one of the source states.
Import	Import lets ClearQuest import records from another source. During Import, ClearQuest validates the contents of imported records. However, ClearQuest does not perform field-level validation during Import. In addition, when a set of state-based records is imported, ClearQuest assigns them to a state specified in the data files without verifying whether they could have legally transitioned to that state. Import actions do not appear in the list of actions in the ClearQuest client.
Modify	Modify lets users modify field values in a record without moving the record between states. Modify actions appear in the list of actions in the ClearQuest client.
Record_script_alias	Record_script_alias lets you associate an action with a record script. Record_script_alias actions appear in the list of actions in the ClearQuest client; this gives you the flexibility to run basically any script you want and associate it with a record in the database.
Submit	Submit enters a new record into the ClearQuest user database. For state-based records, Submit assigns a destination state; the action does not require a source. Each record type can have only one action whose type is Submit.
Unduplicate	Unduplicate is available for state-based record types. Unduplicate removes the link between duplicate records.

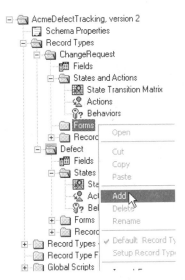

Figure 8–15 *Adding new forms*

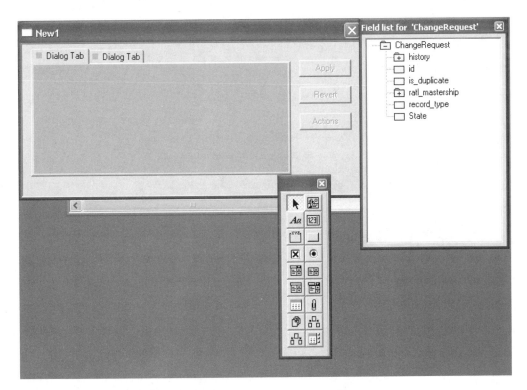

Figure 8–16 *Adding New Forms editor*

access to what records. Then look inside the use cases for the classes being used.

Permissions to view and edit the user interface are limited to the tabs of the individual forms that you create. In order to use this feature, you need to create user groups; this will help you set the permissions on the individual tabs. (See Working with Users and Roles in Chapter 7 for information about user groups.)

To set permissions for a tab, click on the tab, then right-click and select Tab Properties (Figure 8–17).

A window appears showing the properties of the given tab. You can change the permissions for the tab using this window, as shown in Figure 8–18.

Choose All Users if you want to allow all users to have access to this tab; otherwise, choose only those groups for which you want to provide access.

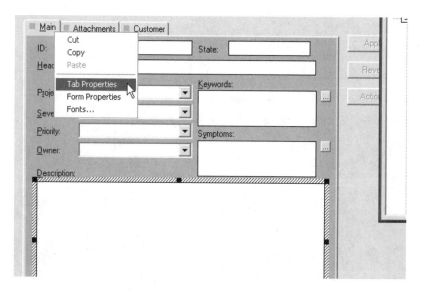

Figure 8–17   *Selecting Tab Properties*

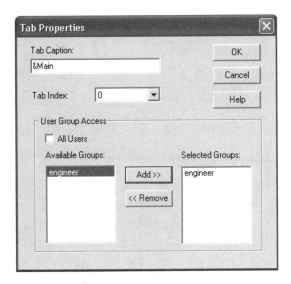

Figure 8–18   *Tab Properties window*

Adding Fields to a Form

Tabs are not useful without any associated information or controls. So, you may want to add fields from the given record for this tab. Looking at the use cases again, you can easily find which tabs you need to create and what fields you need to put on each tab. The fields available for the tab are found in the Field List popup, as shown in Figure 8–19.

Figure 8–19   *Available tab fields*

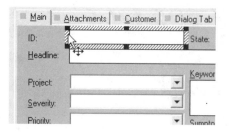

Figure 8–20   *Double-clicking a field to edit*

Basically, you can drag and drop the fields from the Available Tab Fields popup onto the drawing area for the tab. The type of field will dictate what kind of field input control will be used. Each field that you add comes with an input text box and a label. Depending on the type of field, ClearQuest will change different properties of the text input. The best way to see and change the text input field is to double-click on the input box, as shown in Figure 8–20.

Double-clicking will cause ClearQuest to display the dialog box shown in Figure 8–21.

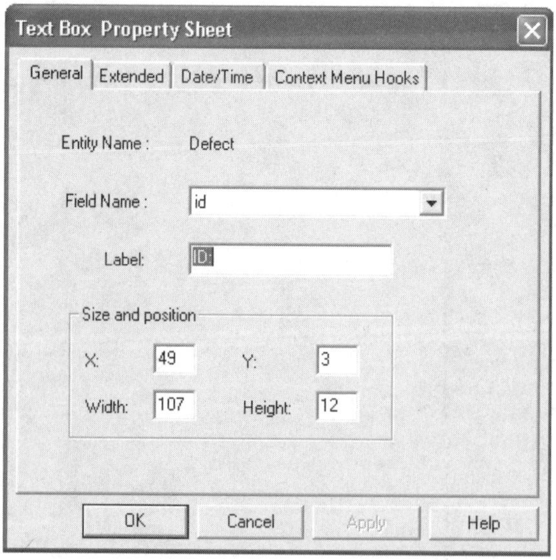

Figure 8–21   *General tab of the Text Box Property Sheet window*

Notice that there are four tabs for the properties of the text box for the given field. The General tab also contains the name of the field and the name of the label for the text box.

Now click on the Extended tab (Figure 8–22). This tab displays information about the text box and allows you to establish different characteristics.

Now click on the Date/Time tab (Figure 8–23). If the field is a date/time field, then the Date and Time check boxes should already be checked. You can select what type of date format to use.

Now click on the Context Menu Hooks tab (Figure 8–24). This tab lets you add shortcuts to hooks (in other words, record hooks to the context menu of a control). This means that at runtime, a user can execute these hooks by right-clicking the control and selecting the hook.

You can associate as many hooks as are available with the control. To associate a hook, simply select the hook in the Available list and click

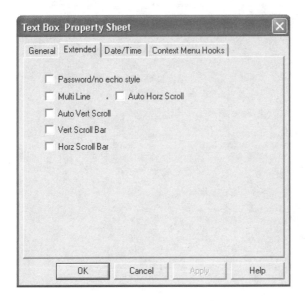

Figure 8–22   *Extended tab*

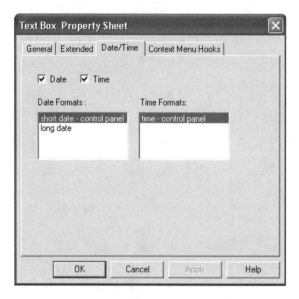

Figure 8–23   *Date/Time tab*

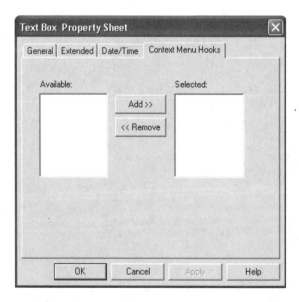

Figure 8–24   *Context Menu Hooks tab*

Add. To remove a hook, select it from the Selected list and click Remove.

Adding Available Controls

Fields are not the only things that you can add to a tab. You can add several different controls for the sake of user assistance. Table 8–3 presents the controls available in ClearQuest, as listed in the ClearQuest Designer's Guide.

Each control also has properties specific to it. You can find details about these controls in the ClearQuest Designer's Guide.

Validating User Input in Fields

Many times you will want to validate the input the user has given. You want to make sure that the presented value is within a specific range of valid values, is in the correct format, or matches a list of items in the database.

You can perform many kinds of validation on fields on a form. The thing to realize here is that the validation is not done on the actual user interface element but on the field itself. First, in the schema browser, select the Fields item (Figure 8–25).

As you can see in Figure 8–26, to the right, you can select the Validation box for the individual field for which validation should be written.

Next, you need to choose the language in which you would like to write the validation script. When you do this, an editor with the chosen language will appear.

The general rule on the script languages is to return a string when the field value change is not valid and to return an empty string if the input value is valid.

Table 8–3 *ClearQuest Controls*

Form Control	Description
ActiveX	Incorporates any registered ActiveX control into a form. You write the initialization record script and the action record script.
Attachment	Displays a list of attached files and includes a set of controls that allow users to add, remove, or view attached files.
Check Box	Is a two-value control used for Boolean values or any field that has only two values. To specify the two values, right-click the control on the form and select Properties.
Combo Box	Combines an editable text field with a list box.
Dropdown Combo Box	Combines an editable text field with a dropdown list box.
Dropdown List Box	Displays a list of possible values for a particular field.
Duplicate Box	Displays the ID of the record of which this record is a duplicate.
Duplicate Dependent	Displays the IDs of any records that are duplicates of this record.
Group Box	Visually groups one or more other controls.
History	Displays information about the actions that have been applied to a record.
List Box	Displays a list of possible values for a particular field. List boxes include an additional control for selecting one or more items from a choice list.
List View	Allows you to display the records associated with a field of the REFERENCE_LIST type. Displays the associated reference list in a multi-column format.
Option Button	Is used in groups to represent a set of mutually exclusive choices. Option buttons allow the selection of only one option in a group.
Parent/Child	Allows you to set up a form to link associated records. These are used with the REFERENCE_LIST field type. The parent/child control consists of both a list view control and three pushbuttons. The list view control and pushbuttons are automatically associated using a unique list view ID. If you change the ID of the list view, you must also update the pushbuttons.
Picture	Allows you to display a static image on your form.
Pushbutton	Initiates specific tasks related to the record. You can associate pushbuttons with record hooks or with list views.
Static Text	Displays an uneditable text string.
Text Box	Displays a field's value as an editable text string.

Figure 8–25   *Selecting the Fields item for validation*

Here is an example written in BASIC:

```
Function resolution_Validation(fieldname)
    ' fieldname As String
    ' resolution_Validate As String
    Dim value
    Set value = GetFieldValue(fieldname)
    If Len(value.GetValue > 10 Then
        resolution_Validation = "Must be smaller than 10
            characters"
    End If
End Function
```

And here is one written in Perl:

```
sub resolution_Validation
{
    my ($pFieldName) = @_;
    my $theRetVal;
    my $theValue = $entity->GetFieldValue($pFieldName)
      ->GetValue();
    if(length($theValue) > 10)
    {
```

Field Name	Type	Default Value	Permission	Value Changed	Validation	Choice List
Resolution_Statetype	STATETYPE					
Resolution	SHORT_STRING		BASIC,PERL		PERL	CONSTANT_LIST
Attachments	ATTACHMENT_LIST					N/A
Project	REFERENCE					DEFAULT
customer_severity	SHORT_STRING					CONSTANT_LIST

Figure 8–26   *Selecting Validation Box for Field*

```
        $theRetVal = "Must be smaller than 10 characters";
    }
    return $theRetVal;
}
```

Hook Scripting

[S.8.3–S.8.11] It is important to understand where and how to use the hooks that ClearQuest provides the designer. To completely cover this topic would require a book of its own. So we'll just cover the basic concepts of what you can do with hooks—just what is important for your initial deployment. There are two basic types of hooks: action hooks and field hooks.

Action Hooks

[A.8.5] *Action hooks* are used to initiate actions that occur for transitions, and also for other general actions. There are several areas where hooks can be called as a result of certain actions being called. Table 8–4, culled from the ClearQuest Designer's Guide, presents a list of hooks for specific actions.

Field Hooks

[S.8.12–S.8.16] *Field hooks* are used to work with fields such as validation, value changes, and pretty much anything else that has to do with fields. Table 8–5, also based on information in the ClearQuest Designer's Guide, shows just when and how to use these hooks.

One Last Thing

[T.8.1] Our good friend Tom Milligan over at IBM, upon reviewing the first draft of this book, reminded us that when you are defining a schema for ClearQuest, you will probably need to take into account

Table 8–4 *Action Hooks*

Action Hook	Operation	When Run
Access control	Returns a Boolean indicating whether the specified user can initiate the specified action on a record. This hook is called before the user performs the action. You can write an access control hook as a VBScript or Perl subroutine. **Note**: To run a primary action (modify, submit, delete, import), the current user must be in the access control list for the primary action as well as for all the base actions.	When the action is about to start
Initialization	Sets initial field values (or any task you specify). Allows complex initialization of a record. You can use this hook to set up field values before ClearQuest begins an action. This hook is called after the action has been initialized but before the contents of the record are displayed in a form. You must write an initialization hook as a script subroutine.	When the action starts
Validation	Validates the field values you specify. If the user types invalid data, ClearQuest prompts the user for valid data. You can use this hook to check conditions that are difficult to verify inside the individual field validation hooks. For example, you can use this hook to verify information across a group of fields. ClearQuest runs this hook before committing any changes to the database. Validation hooks must use a script.	When the user commits the action
Commit	Links an action on multiple records into a single transaction (e.g., resolving all the duplicates of a change request when the original is resolved). Updates a set of external data sources so that they stay parallel with the database contents. This hook is called after changes are added to the database but before those changes are committed. You can write a commit hook as a VBScript or Perl subroutine.	Just before ClearQuest commits the transaction to the database
Notification	Starts a postcommit action that notifies users when an action is performed. Notification hooks must use a script.	After ClearQuest commits the transaction

Table 8–5 *Field Hooks*

Field Hook	Description
Choice list	Returns a set of legal values. Use this hook with fields that are displayed using a list-type control, such as a list box or combo box.
	You can also provide values without scripting by using a constant or a dynamic list.
Default value	Sets the initial value of the field. This hook is called at the beginning of a Submit action.
	You can write a default value hook with a script subroutine. You can also assign a constant value as the default value.
Permission	Returns one of the BehaviorType constants indicating the user's access to the field. Use this hook to force workflow and/or security. (See the online *API Reference for Rational ClearQuest* for enumerated constants.)
	If you add a permission hook to a field, you must modify the Behaviors grid so that at least one of the field's behaviors is set to USE_HOOK. Failure to do this will result in a validation error.
Validation	Validates the contents of the field. This hook is called when the value changes, to provide the user with immediate feedback regarding the validity of the field's contents before committing the record to the database.
Value changed	Responds to changes in the value of a field. Use this hook to trigger updates for other fields (e.g., dependent lists).
	After executing this hook, ClearQuest validates any field the script has modified by calling the field's validation hook (if any).

any existing change request data. This data needs to be imported into ClearQuest. No matter what kind of schema you create, you need to ensure that the right data types are created and assigned for all of the data you import. Make the wrong assignments or mislabel your data types, and your data import will most likely fail.

Tom wrote a nice little utility to help with the data type assignment process, which you can find online at http://www-128.ibm.com/developerworks/rational/library/4332.html/.

Thanks for pointing that out, Tom!

developerWorks Links

A.8.1	http://www-128.ibm.com/developerworks/rational/library/1045.html
A.8.2	http://www-128.ibm.com/developerworks/rational/library/4268.html
S.8.1	http://www-128.ibm.com/developerworks/rational/library/4512.html
S.8.2	http://www-128.ibm.com/developerworks/rational/library/3864.html
A.8.3	http://www-128.ibm.com/developerworks/rational/library/3849.html
A.8.4	http://www-128.ibm.com/developerworks/rational/library/5224.html
S.8.3	http://www-128.ibm.com/developerworks/rational/library/4494.html
S.8.4	http://www-128.ibm.com/developerworks/rational/library/4388.html
S.8.5	http://www-128.ibm.com/developerworks/rational/library/4557.html
S.8.6	http://www-128.ibm.com/developerworks/rational/library/4354.html
S.8.7	http://www-128.ibm.com/developerworks/rational/library/4434.html
S.8.8	http://www-128.ibm.com/developerworks/rational/library/4358.html
S.8.9	http://www-128.ibm.com/developerworks/rational/library/4367.html
S.8.10	http://www-128.ibm.com/developerworks/rational/library/4372.html
S.8.11	http://www-128.ibm.com/developerworks/rational/library/4236.html
A.8.5	http://www-128.ibm.com/developerworks/rational/library/2770.html
S.8.12	http://www-128.ibm.com/developerworks/rational/library/4410.html

S.8.13   http://www-128.ibm.com/developerworks/rational/
           library/05/517_doren/
S.8.14   http://www-128.ibm.com/developerworks/rational/
           library/4351.html
S.8.15   http://www-128.ibm.com/developerworks/rational/
           library/3911.html
S.8.16   http://www-128.ibm.com/developerworks/rational/
           library/4437.html
T.8.1   http://www-128.ibm.com/developerworks/rational/
           library/5817.html

9

ClearQuest for Eclipse

[A.9.1, A9.2] **Eclipse** is a free software/open source platform-independent software framework for delivering what the project calls "rich-client applications," as opposed to "thin client" browser-based applications. So far this framework has typically been used to develop IDEs (Integrated Development Environments), such as the highly regarded Java IDE called Java Development Toolkit (JDT) and compiler that comes as part of Eclipse (and which are also used to develop Eclipse itself). However, it can be used for other types of client application as well. See the popular BitTorrent client Azureus for example.

Eclipse was originally developed by IBM as the successor of its VisualAge family of tools. Eclipse is now managed by the Eclipse Foundation, an independent not-for-profit consortium of software industry vendors. Many notable software tool vendors have embraced Eclipse as a future framework for their IDEs, among them Borland, BEA Systems and IBM Rational.

—Wikipedia[1]

---

1. http://en.wikipedia.org/wiki/Eclipse_%28software%29.

[A.9.3] One of the newest features of ClearQuest is the Eclipse plug-in, which allows you to take full advantage of the Eclipse interface for multisite teams. Eclipse began as an IBM project; in late 2003, an IBM-independent foundation was formed to further the development of Eclipse. Here's a quick overview from the Eclipse Foundation website.

> The Eclipse technology is a vendor-neutral, open development platform supplying frameworks and exemplary, extensible tools. Eclipse Platform tools are exemplary in that they verify the utility of the Eclipse frameworks, illustrate the appropriate use of those frameworks, and support the development and maintenance of the Eclipse Platform itself; Eclipse Platform tools are extensible in that their functionality is accessible via documented programmatic interfaces. The purpose of Eclipse Foundation Inc. is to advance the creation, evolution, promotion, and support of the Eclipse Platform and to cultivate both an open source community and an ecosystem of complementary products, capabilities, and services.
>
> Eclipse has formed an independent open eco-system around royalty-free technology and a universal platform for tools integration. Eclipse based tools give developers freedom of choice in a multi-language, multi-platform, multi-vendor environment. Eclipse provides a plug-in based framework that makes it easier to create, integrate and utilize software tools, saving time and money. By collaborating and exploiting core integration technology, tool producers can leverage platform reuse and concentrate on core competencies to create new development technology. The Eclipse Platform is written in the Java language and comes with extensive plug-in construction toolkits and examples. It has already been deployed on a range of development workstations including Linux, HP-UX, AIX, Solaris, QNX, Mac OS X and Windows based systems.[2]

A history of the Eclipse Foundation's charter is available at the website as well.

Before you jump into the Eclipse client, we'll share a few of the pros and cons to this solution.

In favor of the Eclipse client are the following benefits.

---

2. http://www.eclipse.org/org/.

- Your developers can use the same tool for development as they use to track defects.

- They can easily change Eclipse tasks into trackable tasks within ClearQuest.

- One tool is easier to manage and maintain.

- The Eclipse client can have multiple ClearQuest login sessions open simultaneously—something the native Windows Clear-Quest client cannot do.

On the other hand, consider these issues.

- The Eclipse client requires a lot of memory (buy stock in memory manufacturers).

- It can—and does—slow down Eclipse on underpowered machines (due to a lack of memory and CPU speed).

- It's yet another tool to manage and maintain. While this seems to rebuff one of the items on the list of pros, just remember that setting things up on hundreds of machines can be difficult to manage.

- The Eclipse client doesn't currently allow the "drilldown" into chart data that the native Windows client provides.

As with any new tool or architectural decision, make sure you understand all of the issues before you make a technical and financial commitment.

Installing and Configuring the ClearQuest Plug-in

The first step is downloading and installing the plug-in onto your system. You can download the GA (general availability) version of Rational ClearQuest Client for Eclipse at http://www-1.ibm.com/support.

Connecting to Databases

Before you can use the ClearQuest Eclipse plug-in, you *must* connect to a ClearQuest database. To connect and log in to a database, you will need to follow along with the steps in the Login Wizard. The wizard walks through the process of logging into a connection; you can invoke it from the ClearQuest Navigator view (1), the Eclipse main toolbar (2), or the ClearQuest menu (3), as shown in Figure 9–1.

[S.9.1] Once you have chosen one of these three methods, a Login Wizard dialog will appear. The first page will prompt you for a schema repository (Figure 9–2). A combo box shows all the available schema repositories. Select the schema repository you wish to connect to and click Next.

Now the wizard will prompt you for a user ID (Figure 9–3). This is the user ID for the database that contains the schema repository. Don't forget to click Finish to complete execution of the wizard.

Another dialog will pop up that will prompt you for the password and database to connect to (Figure 9–4).

The "Remember the password" option allows you to save the password for subsequent logins. If you select this option, ClearQuest encrypts and stores the password and uses it on subsequent logins.

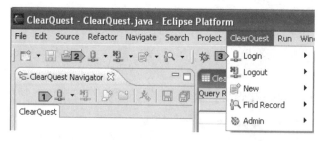

Figure 9–1 *Accessing the Login Wizard*

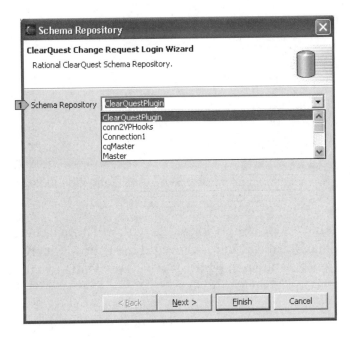

Figure 9–2   *Schema Repository window*

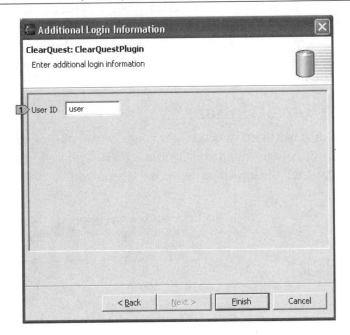

Figure 9–3   *Additional Login Information window*

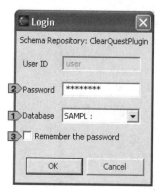

Figure 9–4   *Authentication dialog*

Once you have successfully logged in, you will notice changes to the Eclipse ClearQuest Navigator view and the Eclipse ClearQuest Query Results view. As shown in Figure 9–5, a new ClearQuest tab is added to the ClearQuest Navigator view.

The connection information is also shown in the ClearQuest Navigator view (2). You can expand the connection information node to view the public and personal queries. Note also that the ClearQuest Query Results view title has been changed to reflect the connection information based on your last successful login. The connection that you created using the Login Wizard is persisted for future use.

Setting E-mail Options

[S.9.2–S.9.6] The ClearQuest Eclipse plug-in also allows you to perform a couple of administrative options while still inside Eclipse: changing e-mail options and changing user profiles.

Figure 9–5   *ClearQuest Navigator Tab*

Just as with the native client, changing the e-mail options enables notifications when actions are performed. As shown in Figure 9–6, you start the E-mail Options Wizard by going to the main menu and selecting ClearQuest → Admin → E-mail Options.

The wizard has two pages that walk you through changing your e-mail options. The first page allows you to change e-mail provider information; the second page allows you to configure the e-mail provider. Make sure that you click Finish to apply the changes you have made. ClearQuest will make your changes available right away.

User Profiles

User profiles contain information about your users, including login names, full user names, passwords, e-mail addresses, and phone numbers. You can edit user information using the ClearQuest Eclipse plug-in. To access the user profile and make changes, select Clear-Quest → Admin → Change User Profile from the main menu (Figure 9–7).

The User Profile dialog will appear (Figure 9–8). This dialog allows you to modify the password, full name, e-mail, and phone number of the logged-in user. (This is the only user for whom you can change information.) ClearQuest immediately applies changes you make to the user profile to the User database.

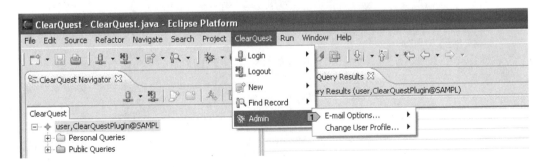

Figure 9–6   *Changing e-mail options*

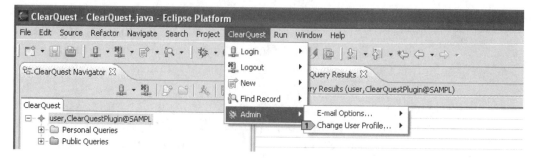

Figure 9–7   *Accessing user profiles*

Considerations for ClearQuest MultiSite

ClearQuest MultiSite is supported within the ClearQuest Eclipse plug-in. You perform basic actions in the same way as you do within a non-multisite environment, except available actions are restricted depending on mastership. This is shown with a lock icon in all of the Eclipse views that show ClearQuest record information (Figure 9–9).

Workspace objects in the ClearQuest Navigator view display mastership information with the addition of a lock icon.

The Query Results view, as shown in Figure 9–10, displays mastership information in an additional column. Again, a lock icon indicates the record is mastered remotely.

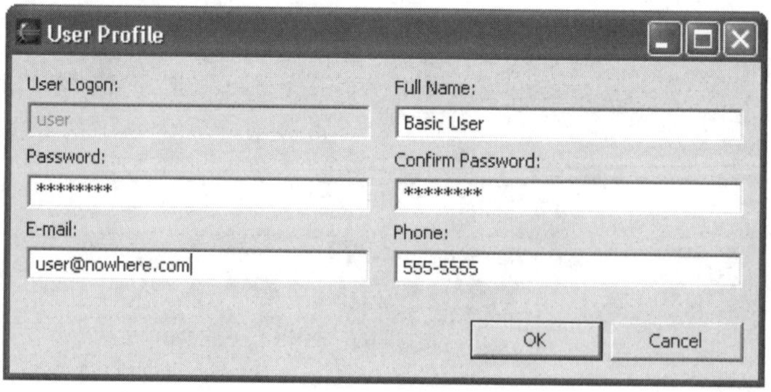

Figure 9–8   *User Profile window*

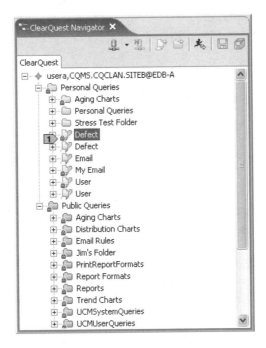

Figure 9–9   *Restricted records*

id	Headline	ratl_mastership	State
EDB-A000000	spelling error in login screen	SITEA	Opened
EDB-A00000004	want more help on inventory report	SITEA	Resolved
EDB-A00000005	columns out of alignment - step 28	SITEB	Resolved
EDB-A00000006	delete item not working correctly	SITEB	Opened
EDB-A00000007	override price does not work	SITEB	Resolved
EDB-A00000008	alt-C does not invoke cancel operation	SITEA	Resolved
EDB-A00000009	inventory re-order not done on large sale	SITEA	Resolved
EDB-A00000010	logout button should be disabled during sale	SITEB	Resolved
EDB-A00000011	change due amount is supposed to be red	SITEB	Assigned
EDB-A00000012	would like logout button to be larger	SITEB	Submitted
EDB-A00000014	oooooooooo	SITEA	Resolved
EDB-A00000015	end-of-shift report fails if after midnight	SITEA	Resolved
EDB-A00000016	too many spaces in "change due" field	SITEA	Submitted
EDB-A00000017	delete operation leaves blank line in form	SITEA	Resolved
EDB-A00000018	>>>>>>>>>>><<<<<<<<<<<<<<<<	SITEA	Resolved
EDB-A00000019	sales tax incorrect for NH	SITEA	Submitted
EDB-A00000020	credit card refused message is unclear	SITEA	Resolved
EDB-A00000021	inventory report is not running correctly	SITEA	Assigned
EDB-A00000022	delete item button deletes two items	SITEA	Resolved
EDB-A00000023	request change due in larger font	SITEA	Resolved
EDB-A00000024	overriding price operation allows negative number	SITEA	Submitted
EDB-A00000025	heading of application looks too crowded	SITEB	Resolved
EDB-A00000026	part number column not wide enough	SITEB	Opened
EDB-A00000028	wwwwwwwwwwwwwwwwwwwwwwwwww	SITEA	Submitted
EDB-A00000029	formatting does not look right in inventory report	SITEA	Submitted
EDB-A00000030	AAAAAAAAAAAAAAAAAA	SITEA	Assigned

Query: Personal Queries/Defect | Type: Defect | Total: 52 | Selected: 1

Figure 9–10   *Query Results view*

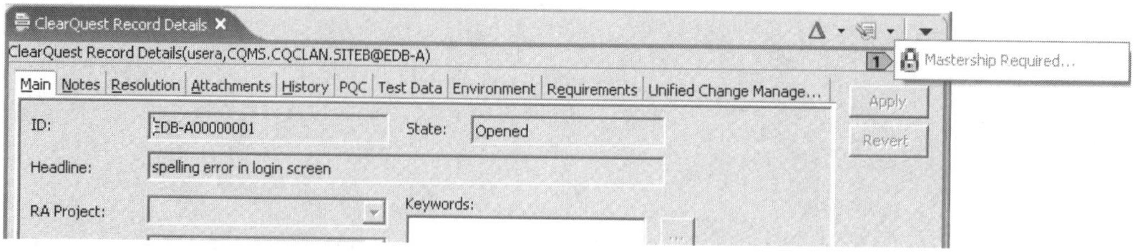

Figure 9–11   *Record Details view*

Mastership for records in the ClearQuest Record Details view, as shown in Figure 9–11, is not apparent. In fact, you will only be notified when you try to perform a Record action and ClearQuest displays "Mastership Required," which indicates that the record is mastered remotely. (This, of course, is not the ideal way to find out something is not writable but is the only one currently available.)

ClearQuest Eclipse Plug-in Preferences

As with most Eclipse plug-ins, the ClearQuest plug-in allows you to customize some of the behavior of the plug-in. To access the preferences, select Window → Preferences from the Eclipse menu bar. Navigate to the Team → ClearQuest node and expand it. An additional Rational ClearQuest Preferences page appears.

There are two Preferences windows available to change: the Rational Defect and Change Tracking window (Figure 9–12) and the Rational ClearQuest Advanced window (Figure 9–13). The Advanced window contains configuration items that help the plug-in display records more effectively.

The defaults in these Preferences windows are typically good enough to run the application sufficiently. You will want to make changes to the preferences if performance is an issue or if you want something other than the default look and feel of the plug-in.

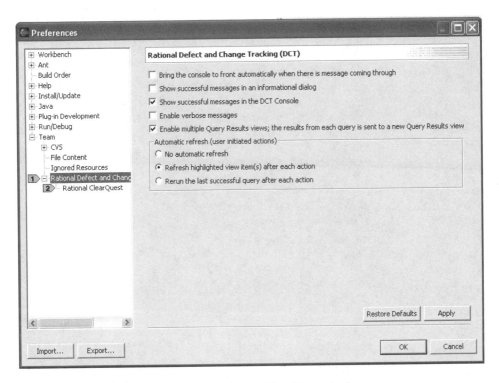

Figure 9–12 *Rational Defect and Change Tracking window*

Using the Plug-in

Eclipse has two pervasive ideas: views and perspectives.

Views show the project, or more specifically the data in the project, in different ways. For example, there is typically a Navigator or Explorer view that shows the files in the file system, and an Editor view that shows the contents of the file.

Perspectives are made up of one or more views. Perspectives can be switched back and forth, in order to reveal different views of the same data.

You can easily create custom views by adding views to a current perspective. Eclipse saves these views in a copy of the perspective to be used at a later time.

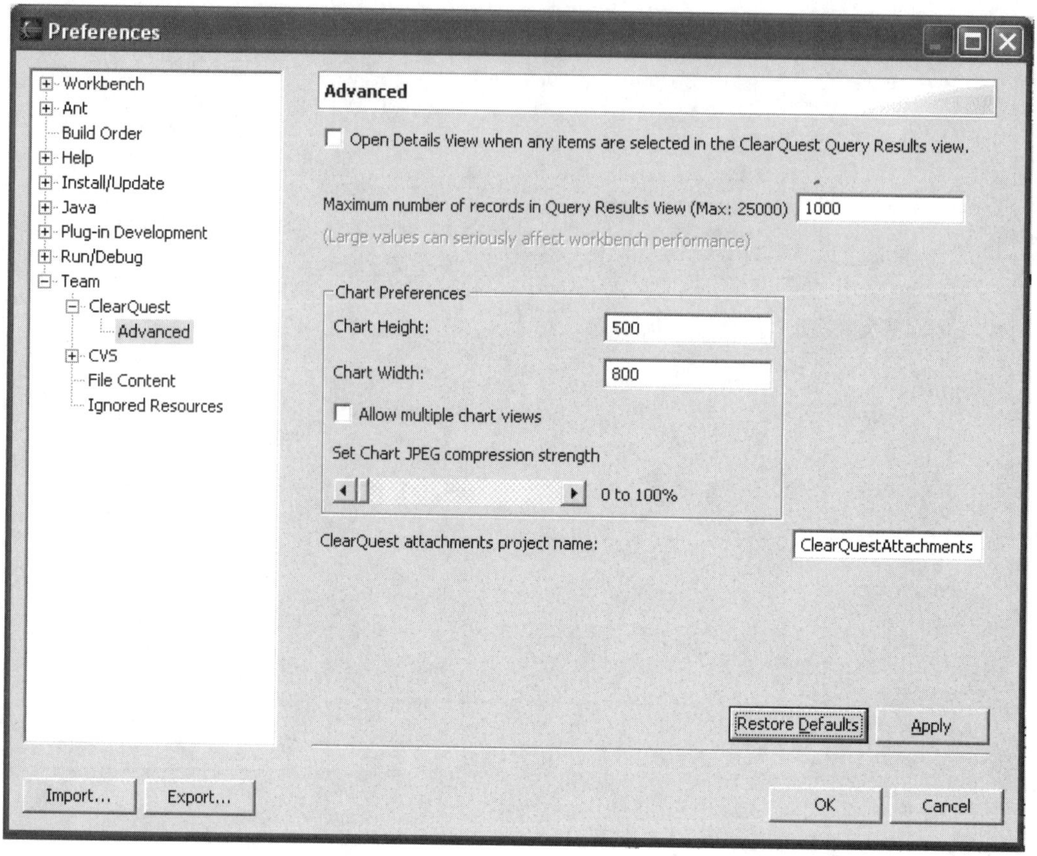

Figure 9–13   *Advanced window*

The ClearQuest Perspective

The ClearQuest plug-in has a perspective for working with ClearQuest in Eclipse. It contains a set of Eclipse views that show ClearQuest data and allows for several ClearQuest actions to be performed (Figure 9–14).

To use the ClearQuest perspective, go to the main menu bar and select Window → Open Perspective → Other → ClearQuest.

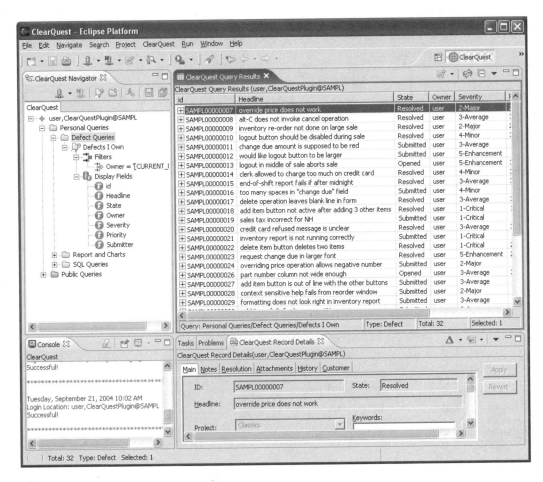

Figure 9–14   *ClearQuest perspective*

ClearQuest Views

The following subsections describe the various views built into
ClearQuest.

ClearQuest Navigator View

The ClearQuest Navigator view, illustrated in Figure 9–15, displays
queries, charts, reports, and report formats.

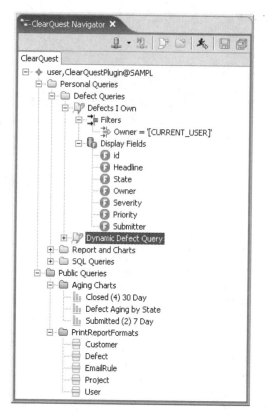

Figure 9–15   *Navigator view*

The Navigator view is analogous to the Workspace view in the Windows client. You can create, modify, rename, delete, and execute queries, reports, and charts. The top-level node in the navigator is named after the connected user and the database to which the user is connected.

The Eclipse ClearQuest Navigator view is very similar to the Workspace view in the ClearQuest native client. However, there are some subtle differences between the two.

- In the Eclipse ClearQuest Navigator, you can view the structure of the workspace object without editing it. For example, you can view the filters and display fields of a query just by expanding a query node.

- Editing components of a workspace object can be performed directly in the Navigator view. You can delete display fields by deleting the corresponding display field node in the Navigator view.

- Auto-generated workspace object names allow you to create copies of workspace objects under the same location. You can copy a query under a folder and paste it under the same folder. The copied query would be assigned an autogenerated name "Copy of {query name}."

ClearQuest Query Results View

The results of queries are displayed in the ClearQuest Query Results view, in a table tree format. You can browse to an associated child record from the parent record.

Figure 9–16 shows how you can expand a defect node to view attachments, history information, and duplicates (1). You can perform actions directly on the records displayed on the query results (2). Selecting multiple records will allow you to perform batch actions on those records.

ClearQuest Record Details View

You can view the details of a record using the ClearQuest Record Details view, as shown in Figure 9–17.

The form is shown exactly as defined by the ClearQuest schema. You can perform actions on the record displayed in the view.

Console View

The Console view is an integral Eclipse view that the Rational ClearQuest plug-in uses to display success and failure messages. You can filter the messages shown in the Console view by using Rational ClearQuest preference settings, as shown in Figure 9–18.

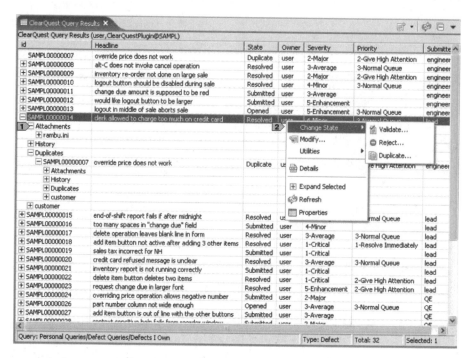

Figure 9–16 *Query Results view*

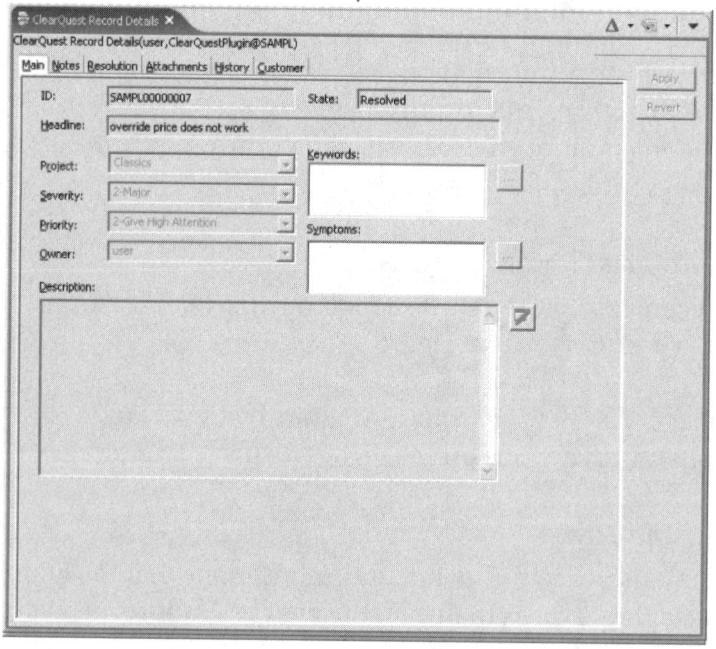

Figure 9–17 *Records Detail view*

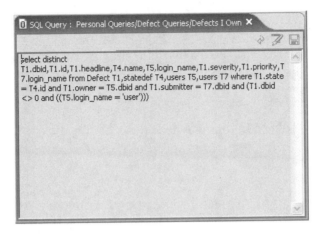

Figure 9–18 *Preference settings*

Tasks View

The Tasks view, shown in Figure 9–19, is an integral Eclipse view that displays the tasks if you are doing any development that uses the default Tasks list in Eclipse. This includes tags in your code like the TODO and FIXME code tags that automatically add tasks to the Tasks view.

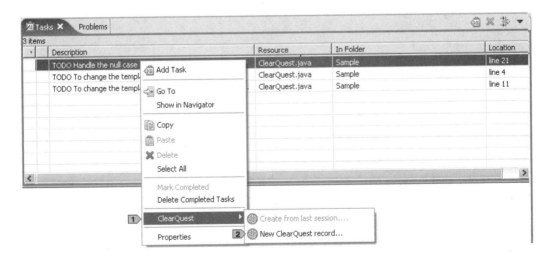

Figure 9–19 *Tasks view*

Alternately, you can create a new task using the Add Task toolbar button and then associate a task with a resource. You can easily turn a task into a ClearQuest record by right-clicking on the task and selecting the ClearQuest menu item (1) and then New ClearQuest Record (2).

Next, a record selection dialog will pop up, listing the connections that are logged into ClearQuest and the types of records that you can create (Figure 9–20).

You can choose to use a logged-in location (1) or create a new location using the New Connection (2) button. Choose the record type (3) and click OK to invoke the new record dialog. The integration automatically populates the Headline and Description fields of the record with task information, provided that the record type has those fields. You can save this type of record and subsequently select it using the same dropdown menu as before.

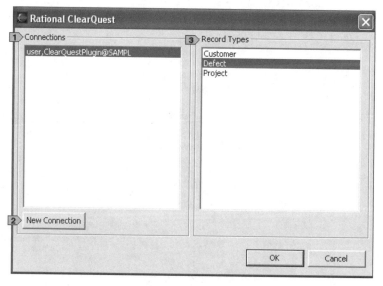

Figure 9–20   *Record selection window*

Queries

The ClearQuest Eclipse plug-in allows you to manage and run queries just like in the native tool. The following subsections show the basic steps involved in working with queries.

Creating a New Query

To create a new query, open the Query Wizard. Then select a folder in the ClearQuest Navigator view within which you want to create the query. Use the context menu (right-click on a folder to view the context menu). Select New Query (Figure 9–21) to invoke the Query Wizard.

You can also invoke the Query Wizard from the New Query toolbar item.

Select the record type and the query name on the Query Name and Record Type page.

The query's Name field is prefilled with a unique query name. The Next button is disabled if you don't choose a record type or if you provide an invalid query name.

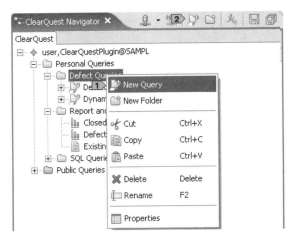

Figure 9–21 *New Query context menu*

What appears as the next page of the wizard depends on whether you select Create Query from an existing query check box (Figure 9–22).

If you wish to create the query from an existing query, enable Create Query from an existing query check box and click on the Next button. You can select an existing query on which you want to base your new query by using the Query Wizard page shown in Figure 9–22.

On the following page (Figure 9–23), you choose the query filters. The valid filter fields for a record type are shown in the left side of the page (1). You can add filters by double-clicking on the filters that are present. You can group the filters added to the right side by using the Group context menu action (2). The context menu actions also allow you to delete filters and groups (3) and change the grouping between And and Or (4). You can set the default filters using the current settings

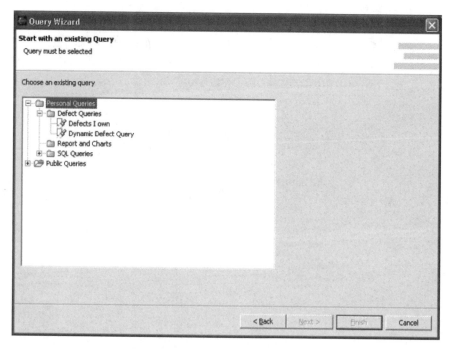

Figure 9–22 *Starting with an existing query*

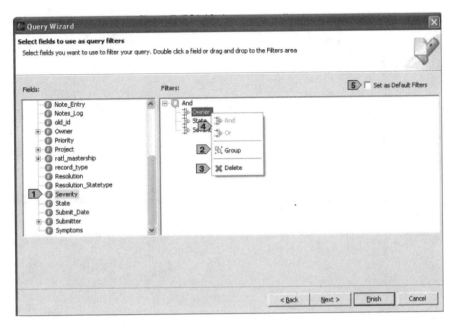

Figure 9–23   *Selecting fields to use as query filters*

by checking the Set as Default Filters check box. By setting this, ClearQuest sets those filters initially for every new query created for that record type.

The Define Query Filters page (Figure 9–24) does not appear if you didn't select a filter on the previous page. You can define the filter values using this page; ClearQuest persists the filter values when you change the selection here.

Choose the display fields in the Define Display Fields page (Figure 9–25).

Add display fields by dragging and dropping the fields (1) or double-clicking on the fields. You can change the title (2), show information for a display field (3), change the sort type (4), or change the sort order (5) by clicking on the appropriate table cell. To run the newly created query, select the Run Query check box (6).

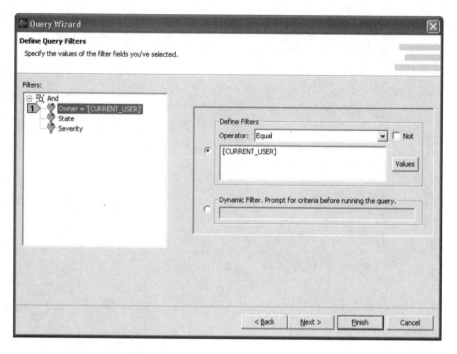

Figure 9–24 *Define Query Filters page*

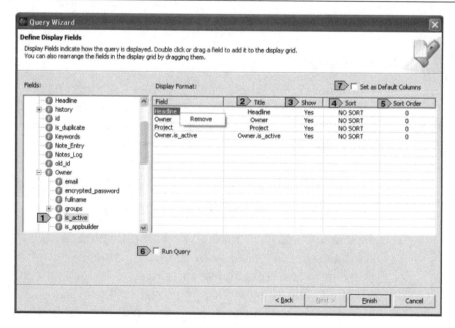

Figure 9–25 *Define Display Fields page*

You can set the default display fields using the current settings by checking the Set as Default Columns check box (7). ClearQuest then initially sets the display fields for every new query created for that record type.

The new query is selected and shown in the ClearQuest Navigator view (Figure 9–26).

The query is decorated with an asterisk decoration (1) to indicate that the query needs to be created or saved in the database. The filters (2) and the display fields (3) contained in a query are shown in the ClearQuest Navigator view, too.

You can also create queries from the ClearQuest main toolbar or the ClearQuest menu. Select New → <connection> → New Query. The first page of this Query Wizard is slightly different. In order to create

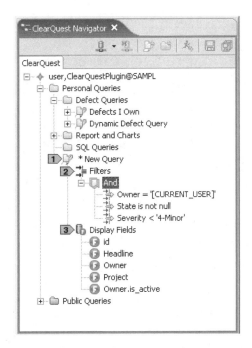

Figure 9–26 *New query shown in the Navigator view*

a query using this wizard, you need to specify the location where the query will be created.

There are some important differences between the ClearQuest Eclipse plug-in and the native Windows client.

- The record type is shown in the first page of the Query Wizard. In the native Rational ClearQuest client, users choose the record type and proceed to choose the filters and display fields in a wizard. This approach does not allow users to change the record type of the query after it has been selected. Within the Eclipse client, the record type is shown in the first page of the wizard. By allowing users to choose the record type as part of the wizard, the client allows you to change the record type even after choosing the filters and display fields corresponding to a different record type.

- The Name field is prefilled with a unique name.

- When you are creating a query based on another query, the page for starting with an existing query is shown only when users choose to create a query from an existing query.

- The filter selection page is shown before the Define Display Fields page. When creating a new query, users usually decide what records are shown before choosing how the records are shown. Hence, the Define Display Fields page is shown after the filter selection page. This also goes hand in hand with a SQL statement where the Select clause (display fields) is shown after the Where (filters) clause.

- The Define Query Filters page is shown only if you selected filters using the filter selection page. This speeds up the creation of queries that return all the records of a particular record type.

- ClearQuest does not automatically save a new query to the server. Unlike the native client, the new query created is not automatically created on the server. An asterisk decoration on the query is added to indicate that the query is not saved to the database. This feature allows users to create temporary queries without saving them to the server.

Editing an Existing Query

You can edit a query by using the Edit Query Wizard. To invoke the Edit Query Wizard, highlight the query and choose Edit (1) from the context menu (Figure 9–27).

The Edit Query Wizard allows users to edit the structure of the query. This wizard shows the Select fields to use as the Query Filters, Define Query Filters, and Define Display Fields pages of the wizard. The asterisk decoration on a query indicates that changes to a query need to be saved to the ClearQuest database.

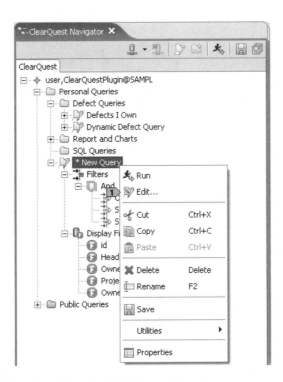

Figure 9–27   *Invoking the Edit Query Wizard*

The ClearQuest Navigator view shows the structure of the query; in other words, the filters and display fields contained under the query appear within the ClearQuest Navigator view. If you want to edit only the filters, you can invoke the Edit Filter Wizard by selecting Edit from the context menu on a filter node. The Select fields to use as the Query Filters page and the Define Query Filters page are the two pages contained in an Edit Filter Wizard. Similarly, to edit the display field, you can invoke the Edit Display Field Wizard by selecting the Edit action on a display field. The Edit Display Field Wizard shows only the Define Display Fields page.

Saving a Query

As discussed earlier, unsaved queries are displayed with an asterisk decoration. To save an unsaved query to the database, highlight the query (1) and select the Save context menu action (2), as shown in Figure 9–28.

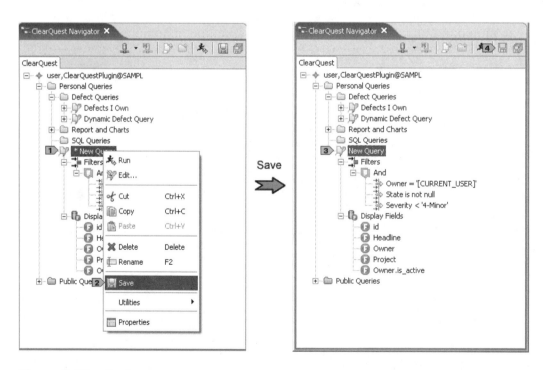

Figure 9–28   *Saving a query*

After the save operation, the asterisk decoration is removed (3), which indicates that the unsaved changes have been committed to the ClearQuest database. You can also save all the unsaved queries belonging to a connection by highlighting the connection node and using the Save All context menu action. (You can also save a query by using the Save toolbar item.)

Renaming or Deleting a Query

You can rename or delete a query using the Rename (1) or Delete (2) actions from the query's context menu, as shown in Figure 9–29.

ClearQuest displays a confirmation dialog that prompts you to confirm a delete operation (but not a rename).

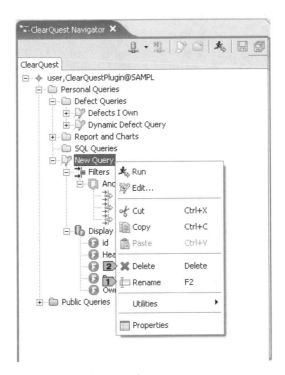

Figure 9–29   *Context menu for deleting or renaming a query*

Viewing the SQL Version of a Query

To view the SQL version of a query, highlight the query and select View SQL from the context menu (1), as shown in Figure 9–30. The SQL is shown in the SQL Query view (2).

You can only edit SQL queries from inside the SQL Query view. To convert a query to a SQL query, highlight the query and select Utilities → View SQL.

Note that you cannot convert a query to a SQL query if you don't have permission to create a new SQL query. The SQL query created by the conversion process is not automatically saved to the server. You can save the query by using the Save Query action. To edit a SQL query, view the SQL of the query by using the View SQL menu action, and select the Edit toolbar button in the SQL Query view. To save the changed SQL statement, use the Save toolbar button in the SQL Query view.

Note that the SQL Query view is not part of the default ClearQuest perspective. You can open the SQL Query view by using Window → Show View → Other → ClearQuest → SQL Query View.

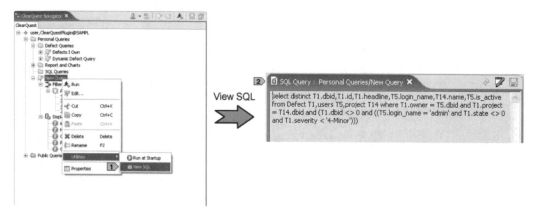

Figure 9–30   *Viewing the SQL version of a query*

Executing a Query on Startup

If you want to execute a query when you connect to a Rational Clear-Quest database, you need to set the query as a startup query. To set the query as a startup query, highlight the query and select Utilities → Run at Startup. A startup query is indicated by the checkmark decoration (1), as shown in Figure 9–31.

To reverse that setting, use Utilities → Run at Startup again. The checkmark is removed when you unset the startup nature of the query. (Note that the beta version of the Rational ClearQuest Client for Eclipse does not allow users to run a chart or a report at startup.)

Executing a Query

There are two ways to execute a query: Double-click on a selected query, or right-click on a query and select the Run action from the context menu. After execution, ClearQuest displays the query results in the ClearQuest Query Results view (Figure 9–32).

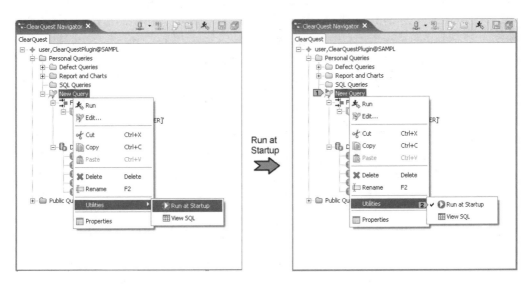

Figure 9–31   *Setting a query to execute on startup*

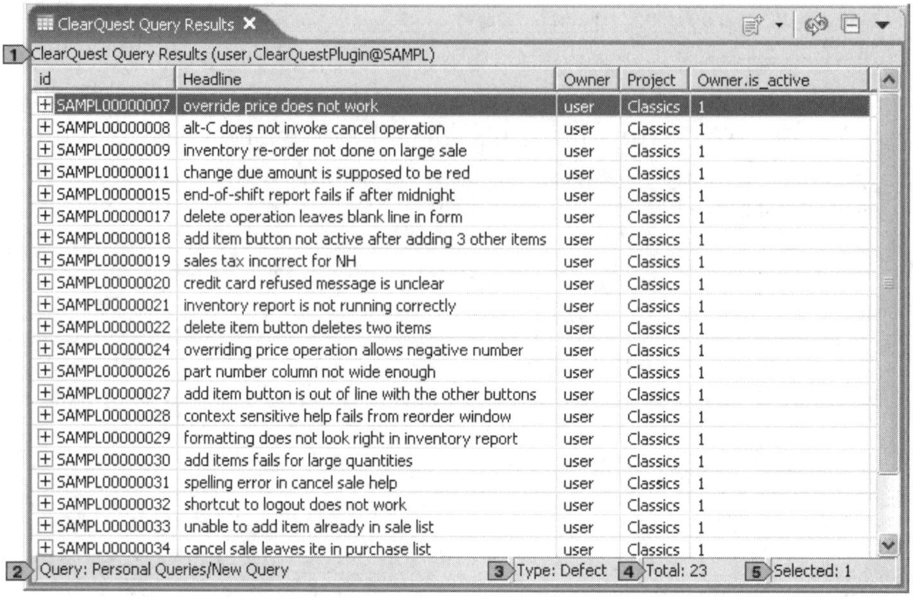

Figure 9–32 *ClearQuest Query Results view*

The columns and the order of the records are formatted according to the query's display field settings. After executing the query, you will notice additional changes in the ClearQuest Query Results view. The database information is displayed in the title of the view (1). The name of the query executed (2), the type of record (3), the number of records returned (4), and the number of selected records (5) appear in the status bar of the Query Results view.

You can expand the records to view the record types referenced by the parent. Expanding the record types further will result in Clear-Quest displaying the referenced records. For example, expanding a defect record will show three nodes: Attachments, Duplicates, and History. Expanding these nodes will show the attachments, duplicates, and history records, respectively, associated with the defect.

If the selected query contains dynamic filters, ClearQuest displays a dynamic query window that you can use to establish the criteria (Figure 9–33).

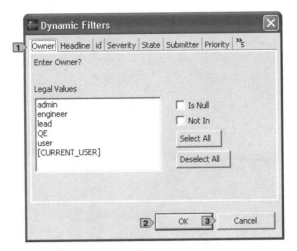

Figure 9–33 *Dynamic Filters window*

The tabs in the Dynamic Filters dialog correspond to the different dynamic filters present in the query (1). Click OK (2) to execute the query based on the criteria set within this dialog. You can cancel the execution of the query by using the Cancel button (3).

The Query Results view displays the query results retrieved by executing the query. To navigate back to the query from the Query Results view, use the Show Query in Navigator menu action.

If the number of results exceeds the maximum results count, a message appears confirming whether or not you want to execute the query. ClearQuest has implemented this measure because executing queries with a large number of results affects the performance adversely. To change the maximum results count, go to the Preferences window.

The Dynamic Filters window can show only a certain number of dynamic filters in the viewing area. If a query contains dynamic filters that can't be accommodated in the viewing area of the Dynamic Filters window, the excess filters are displayed off-screen (1), as shown in Figure 9–34.

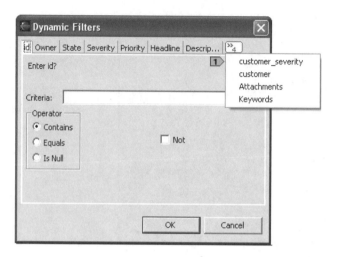

Figure 9–34 *Showing excess filters*

Viewing Multiple Query Results

As we saw in the previous subsection, the results of an executed query are displayed within the ClearQuest Query Results view. Each executed query uses a different ClearQuest Query Results view to display the results. This means that when multiple queries are executed, multiple ClearQuest Query Results views will appear in the ClearQuest perspective.

The location information (1) and the query path name (2) appear in the title of the view and the status bar, respectively (Figure 9–35). When you execute a query, the results are shown in a new ClearQuest Query Results view if there is no such view already associated with the query. The different views are stacked on top of each other.

If a query is executed again, the results will appear in the ClearQuest Query Results view previously assigned to that query. When you log out of a database, ClearQuest automatically closes all the views assigned to queries from that database.

Designating a Rational ClearQuest Query Results view for every executed query is the default behavior of the Rational ClearQuest Client

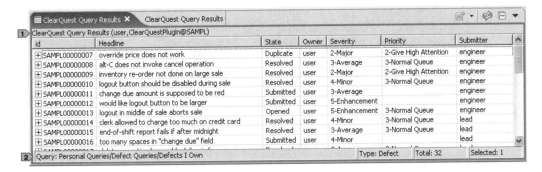

Figure 9–35 *Displaying results for multiple queries*

for Eclipse. You can choose to change the behavior in the Preferences window.

Records

In this section, we look at the actions that you can perform on records using the Rational ClearQuest Client for Eclipse.

Viewing a Record's Information

The ClearQuest Record Details view, shown in Figure 9–36, displays the complete information set for a given record.

To display a record in the ClearQuest Record Details view, select the Details action from the record's context menu. After the Record Details view is displayed, whenever you select a new record, the view will automatically display the information of the record you selected.

The record form is displayed exactly as it was designed in the schema. Selecting different tabs results in ClearQuest displaying the appropriate information. The selected record's database information is shown in the view title (1).

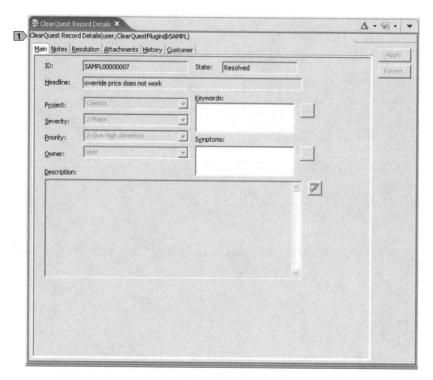

Figure 9–36   *ClearQuest Record Details view*

You can change when and how the ClearQuest Record Details view is shown by changing the preferences.

Performing Actions on a Record

You can perform actions on the records from either the ClearQuest Query Results view or the ClearQuest Record Details view.

Performing Actions from the ClearQuest Query Results View

The ability to perform record actions directly from the ClearQuest Query Results view means that it is very useful to add this view to your development perspective. You can then perform most Clear-Quest activities without changing to the ClearQuest perspective.

In the ClearQuest Query Results view, shown in Figure 9–37, the possible actions for a record are displayed in the record's context menu.

The context menu actions are organized into three categories.

1. *Change State*: Change State actions allow you to transition a record from one state to another.
2. *Modify*: Modify actions allow you to modify the record information.
3. *Utilities*: Utilities actions include Delete and Add Attachment.

When you initiate an action from the menu, the window shown in Figure 9–38 appears.

Fill in the required information and complete the action. The action determines what kind of window appears. For example, a modify form appears when you select the Modify action, while a duplicate action form appears when you initiate a Duplicate action.

You can also perform actions on referenced records (child nodes) from the ClearQuest Query Results view, as shown in Figure 9–39.

The available actions depend on the selected record. You can apply the same action that you perform on a record to multiple records: Highlight the records you want to perform the action on, and then initiate a common action. The usual window will appear, except instead of an Apply button, there is an Apply All button. Click the Apply

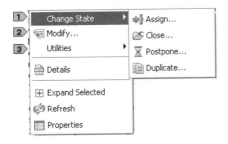

Figure 9–37   *Context menu in the Query Results view*

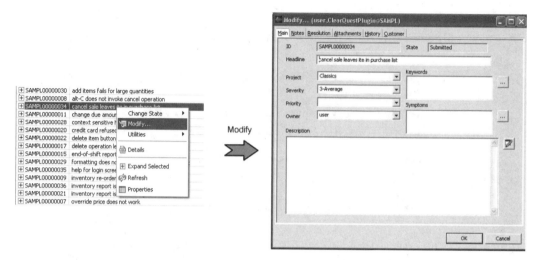

Figure 9–38   *Modifying results in a Modify record window*

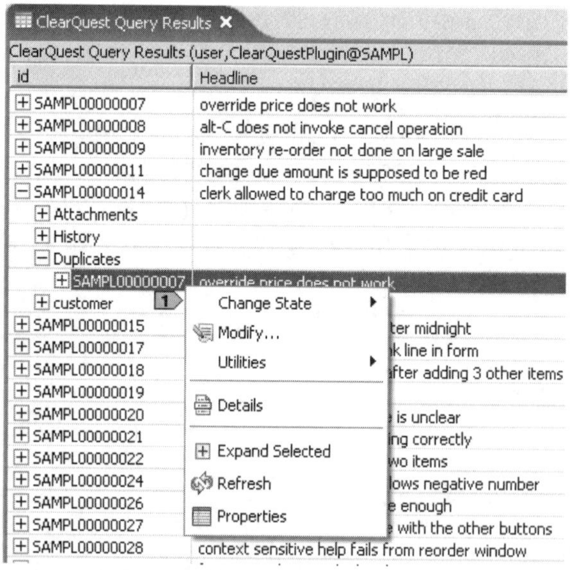

Figure 9–39   *Actions available from a selected record*

All button to tell ClearQuest to perform the action on all of the selected records.

Performing Actions from the ClearQuest Record Details View

In the ClearQuest Record Details view, you perform actions within the view itself rather than from a context menu (Figure 9–40).

The actions are located in the upper-right corner of the view; they are organized in a way similar to the organization within the ClearQuest Query Results view. You initiate actions that are contained in a control (such as attachment actions) from within the form. Other actions, such as Modify, use the record form in the ClearQuest Record Details view to perform the action.

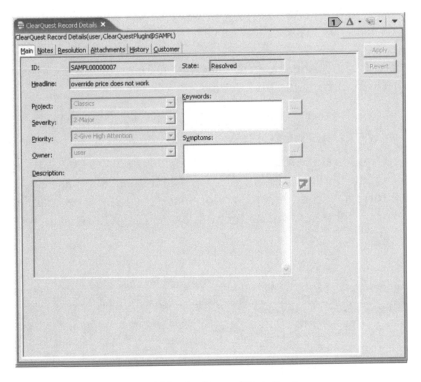

Figure 9–40 *Performing actions within the Record Details view*

Take a look at the Edit icon. You will notice this button next to all multiline text controls. Clicking this icon brings up an edit text dialog, which provides you with a larger, resizable area within which you can edit the text.

Refreshing Records in the ClearQuest Query Results View

ClearQuest refreshes a record within the ClearQuest Query Results view when you perform an action on the record. You can refresh a record manually by right-clicking the record and selecting the Refresh action from the context menu. You can refresh multiple records by using the Refresh action on multiple highlighted records.

You can refresh the entire result set by rerunning the query. You can do this quickly by using the Rerun Query action within the Rational ClearQuest Query Results view toolbar (Figure 9–41).

You can change how the ClearQuest Query Results view is refreshed by modifying the preferences.

Creating Records

Queries are worthless if there are no records to query. If you have create authority in one or more ClearQuest databases, you can perform a "submit record" action using the Eclipse toolbar Submit button or the New menu item under the ClearQuest main menu (Figure 9–42).

Figure 9–41   *Refreshing the query results*

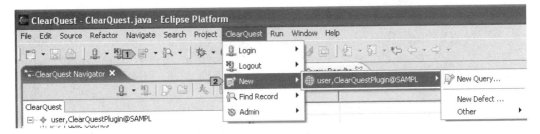

Figure 9–42 *Submitting a new record*

Click on the dropdown menu to display a context menu with active databases. The database you select will determine where the record is created. Expanding the database entry will show the different records you are allowed to create. The state-based record names are displayed as top-level menu actions, while the stateless entries can be accessed via the Other submenu.

Selecting the desired record type results in the appearance of a Create Record window. Fill in the required fields and submit the record.

You can also create records from the ClearQuest Query Results view, as shown in Figure 9–43. The "submit record" action is located within the ClearQuest Query Results view toolbar.

The "create" action allows you to submit records to the database linked to the particular ClearQuest Query Results view. Since you can create records only in the linked database, the context menu displays only record types for that database. In addition, you can click on the main "submit record" action to tell ClearQuest to invoke the submit dialog for the default record type of the current schema.

id	Headline	Owner	Project	Owner.is_active
SAMPL00000007	override price does not work	user	Classics	1

ClearQuest Query Results (user,ClearQuestPlugin@SAMPL)

Figure 9–43 *Submitting new records from the Query Results view*

Finding Records

The Find Record action allows you to retrieve a specific record and view or perform actions on it. This prevents you from having to execute a query just to view or perform actions on a record.

You can initiate this action from either the Find Record button in the Eclipse toolbar or the Find Record menu item under the ClearQuest main menu (Figure 9–44).

The Find Record dialog consists of a dropdown list for choosing the record type (1), a Search All Record Types option (2), an ID search text box (3), and a Check button (4), as shown in Figure 9–45.

You can enter partial identifying strings in the ID text box. Clicking Check tells you what record will be shown based on your ID search string. The record is displayed within the ClearQuest Record Details view.

Working with Record Attachments

[S.9.7, S.9.8] You can open, add, delete, and edit an attachment using the Rational ClearQuest Client for Eclipse. You can perform actions on an attachment from either the ClearQuest Query Results view or the ClearQuest Record Details view. The ClearQuest Query Results

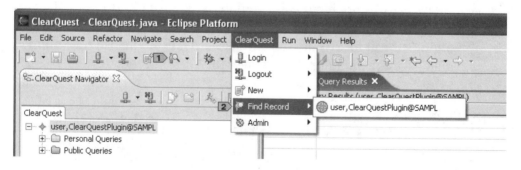

Figure 9–44   *Finding records*

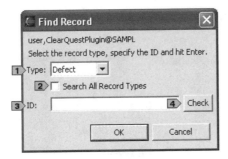

Figure 9–45   *Find Record window*

view shows the attachments as a child node if the particular record type supports attachments.

The following subsections explore the different attachment actions.

Creating an Attachment

To create an attachment, highlight the record and select the Utilities → Add Attachment context menu action (Figure 9–46).

An Add Attachment window appears, allowing you to select the file that needs to be uploaded as an attachment.

Deleting an Attachment

To delete an attachment, highlight the attachment and select the Delete menu action (Figure 9–47).

Figure 9–46   *Adding an attachment*

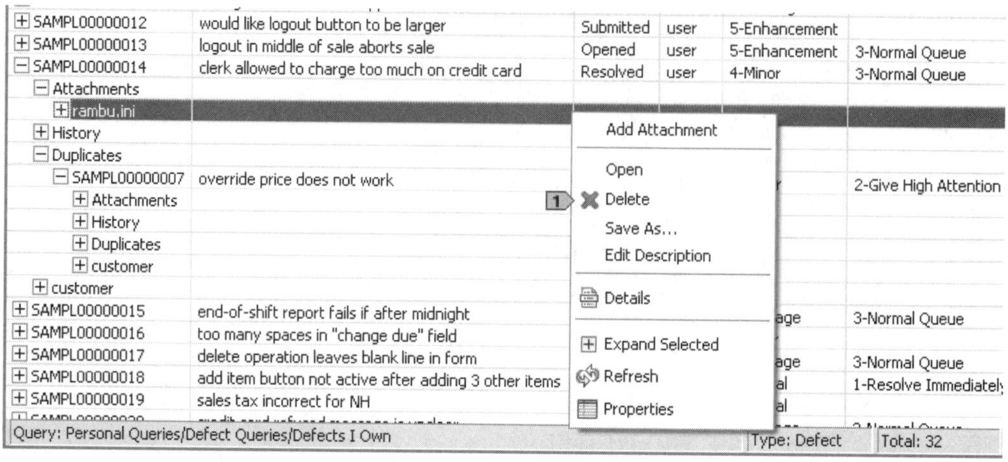

⊞ SAMPL00000012	would like logout button to be larger	Submitted	user	5-Enhancement	
⊞ SAMPL00000013	logout in middle of sale aborts sale	Opened	user	5-Enhancement	3-Normal Queue
⊟ SAMPL00000014	clerk allowed to charge too much on credit card	Resolved	user	4-Minor	3-Normal Queue
⊟ Attachments					
⊞ rambu.ini					
⊞ History					
⊟ Duplicates					
⊟ SAMPL00000007	override price does not work				2-Give High Attention
⊞ Attachments					
⊞ History					
⊞ Duplicates					
⊞ customer					
⊞ customer					
⊞ SAMPL00000015	end-of-shift report fails if after midnight			age	3-Normal Queue
⊞ SAMPL00000016	too many spaces in "change due" field				
⊞ SAMPL00000017	delete operation leaves blank line in form			age	3-Normal Queue
⊞ SAMPL00000018	add item button not active after adding 3 other items			al	1-Resolve Immediately
⊞ SAMPL00000019	sales tax incorrect for NH			al	

Context menu items:
- Add Attachment
- Open
- ✖ Delete
- Save As...
- Edit Description
- 🖨 Details
- ⊞ Expand Selected
- ⟳ Refresh
- 🗒 Properties

Query: Personal Queries/Defect Queries/Defects I Own   Type: Defect   Total: 32

Figure 9–47   *Deleting an attachment*

Opening an Attachment

To open an attachment, highlight the attachment and select Open
from the context menu. The attachment file is temporarily stored
under the ClearQuestAttachment project. You can open the file either in an Eclipse editor or in an external editor. (The value of the
Window → Preferences → Workbench → File Associations preference
determines whether the file is opened inside or outside the Eclipse
shell.) You can modify the file opened in an Eclipse editor or an external editor. When you save the file, the attachment is automatically
saved to the ClearQuest database. ClearQuest automatically deletes
the temporary attachment file when you close the corresponding
editor.

If you prefer to perform attachment actions from the ClearQuest
Record Details view, just initiate the actions from the attachment
control in the form.

developerWorks Links

A.9.1 http://www-128.ibm.com/developerworks/rational/library/04/r-3089/

A.9.2 http://www-128.ibm.com/developerworks/rational/library/content/03July/2500/2834/ClearQuest/CQ_eclipse_plugin092404/readme_clearquest_eclipse.html

A.9.3 http://www-128.ibm.com/developerworks/rational/library/3316.html

S.9.1 http://www-128.ibm.com/developerworks/rational/library/4322.html

S.9.2 http://www-128.ibm.com/developerworks/rational/library/4334.html

S.9.3 http://www-128.ibm.com/developerworks/rational/library/3860.html

S.9.4 http://www-128.ibm.com/developerworks/rational/library/3935.html

S.9.5 http://www-128.ibm.com/developerworks/rational/library/05/517_doren/

S.9.6 http://www-128.ibm.com/developerworks/rational/library/4497.html

S.9.7 http://www-128.ibm.com/developerworks/rational/library/4367.html

S.9.8 http://www-128.ibm.com/developerworks/rational/library/04/r-3179/

10

ClearQuest Integrations

[A.10.1, A.10.2] Turnkey solutions are usually not the end of your deployment efforts; they require further work to refine, extend, and integrate them in order to meet your specific company needs. Then again, just because you can integrate two systems doesn't mean you should integrate them. Thomas Edison was famous for pointing out to visitors of his summer residence the estate's many labor-saving inventions. On the way back to the house, Edison carefully guided his guests to a point in the yard where they had to walk through a curious turnstile that took considerable effort to turn. On a tour of the grounds one day, a guest asked Edison why he had produced such an awkward and cumbersome device. "Well, you see," Edison replied, "everyone who pushes the turnstile around pumps eight gallons of water into the tank on my roof."

While Edison's water tank extension and integration of a turnstyle pumping method may have met his personal lavatory needs, it's often important to take into account all of your user needs when considering ClearQuest integrations and custom development. What makes sense for your own internal operations may not be the best solution for external users. Integrating ClearQuest with other software gives you the ability to deliver a seamless development environment to your user. Of course, IBM Rational provides several integrations with its own products, such as ClearCase and RequisitePro. However, many other companies supply products that may also be a good match for ClearQuest integration.

To understand how to integrate products with ClearQuest, you need to understand some basic concepts. Some ClearQuest integrations are *independent*, meaning they require only adding the appropriate package to your deployment. Other integrations are *dependent*, which means they require you to add not only one or more packages in a specific order but also additional configurations to ClearQuest.

> **Note**: ClearQuest integrations are *not* available to the web client. Therefore, fields, forms, reports, scripts, and other functionality added to the Clear-Quest client by an integration package are *not* available to the web client. Therefore, you must plan before adding packages to your schema. After you add a package to a schema, you cannot remove the package. You must delete all schema versions in which the package exists. You can delete schema versions only if you have not applied them to a user database. *If you are going to allow use of the web client, you need to consider how integrating ClearQuest with another tool will work when someone uses Clear-Quest with the web interface.*

Independent Integrations

The following is a list of independent integrations. Remember: You can use the same installation process for independent integrations as for a standard ClearQuest installation.

- [A.10.3] *Rational ClearCase and ClearQuest*: Associates one or more ClearQuest change requests with one or more ClearCase versions.

- *Rational Purify and ClearQuest*: Allows you to submit data to a ClearQuest database and track it.

- *Rational PurifyPlus and ClearQuest*: Allows you to submit code coverage and performance data to a ClearQuest database and track it.

- *Your e-mail system and ClearQuest*: Enables ClearQuest to communicate with users through their e-mail systems. An e-mail system integration involves configuring Rational E-Mail Reader and adding the e-mail notification package.

Dependent Integrations

The following is a list of dependent integrations. They require adding more than one package to the schema in a specific order and typically require changes to your ClearQuest configuration.

- *Rational Administrator and ClearQuest*: Associates Rational projects with ClearQuest databases.

- *Rational ClearQuest Project Tracker and ClearQuest*: Enables data exchange between ClearQuest and Microsoft Project.

- *Rational RequisitePro and ClearQuest*: Associates RequisitePro requirements with ClearQuest records.

- *Rational TestManager and ClearQuest*: Allows you to submit defects found through TestManager to ClearQuest databases and to track them.

- [A.10.4] *Rational Unified Change Management (UCM) and ClearQuest*: Links ClearCase UCM projects and activities to ClearQuest records.

- *Microsoft Visual SourceSafe and ClearQuest*: Associates Visual SourceSafe information with ClearQuest records.

Adding Packages to Your Schema

In order to use the available integrations or packages just described, you will need to add them to your schema. The best way to accomplish this task is to use the Package Wizard.

To start the Package Wizard, open your schema in ClearQuest Designer and select Package → Package Wizard. The dialog box shown in Figure 10–1 will appear.

This dialog shows the latest versions of the packages that are available and that need to be added to the schema. If a package has aspects that can be applied to a record, then a Next button will appear. For example, look at the AMStateTypes package in Figure 10–2.

Click on the Next button, and then select the records to which the package should be applied. As shown in Figure 10–3, the Enhancement and Defect records will have the AMStateTypes package applied to it.

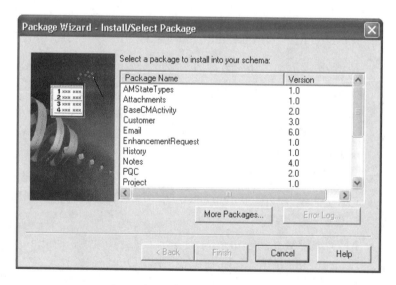

Figure 10–1   *Package Wizard window*

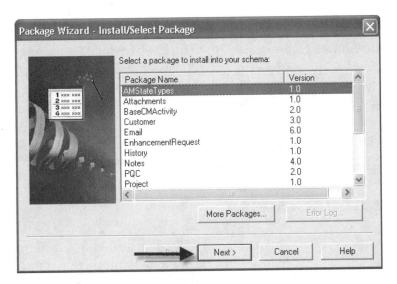

Figure 10–2   *Selecting the AMStateTypes package*

In general, some packages require additional steps. Basically, you should follow the wizard through the steps to install all of the necessary packages. It's fairly straightforward.

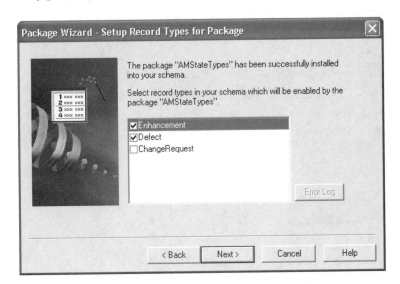

Figure 10–3   *Applying the AMStateTypes package to records*

Enabling Record Types for Integrations

Sometimes you may find that you have installed a package and added additional records by mistake, or you forgot to apply a package to a specific record. Don't worry: You can always apply the package to the record after the fact. To enable package functionality for a new record type, click Package → Setup Record Type for Packages in the ClearQuest Designer with a schema open (Figure 10–4).

ClearQuest Packages

[A.10.5, A.10.6] Several packages can be added to a schema. These packages include functional and data elements that allow for integration with other tools in your change management system and with other critical back-end systems. However, you may find these packages useful even without integration to other tools.

Table 10–1 outlines several different package types and describes whether they add or modify record fields and which fields they impact.

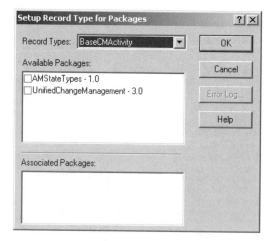

Figure 10–4   *Setup Record Type for Packages window*

Table 10-1 *Common ClearQuest Packages*

Package	Description	Added or Modified	Fields
AMBaseActivity	Provides additional support for Rational ClearQuest Project Tracker.	Adds the Main tab to the forms of the enabled record type.	Headline Owner Description
AMStateTypes	Provides additional support for Rational Unified Change Management (UCM) and its state types. Requires you to map schema states to the following state types: Waiting, Ready, Active, Complete.	Does not add any record types.	am_statetype
AMWorkActivitySchedule	Provides scheduling attributes needed to integrate Rational ClearQuest and Microsoft Project 2000 using Rational ClearQuest Project Tracker. With the AMWorkActivitySchedule record type family, you can query records being created and updated with Rational ClearQuest Project Tracker.	Defines and adds the AMSchedule record type family to the enabled schema. Record types being enabled with this package are added to this record type family. Adds the Schedule tab to the enabled record type.	am_planned_start_date am_planned_end_date am_planned_work am_planned_rem_work am_planned_duration am_planned_rem_duration am_actual_start_date am_actual_end_date am_actual_work
Attachments (read-only)	Lets you add and remove attachments related to a record.	Adds an Attachments tab to the enabled record type.	Attachments
BaseCMActivity	Provides support for the BaseCMActivity record type, which is included in the UCM and Enterprise schemas as a lightweight activity record type. You can use this alternative to the Defect record type as is, enable it for UCM, or develop it into a new record type. For more information, see *Managing Software Projects with Rational ClearCase.*	Adds the BaseCMActivity record type.	Owner Description Headline

(continued)

189

Table 10-1 *Common ClearQuest Packages (Continued)*

Package	Description	Added or Modified	Fields
CharacterSet Validation	Prevents data corruption by validating that all data entered into a record from the native client is from the same code page as the ClearQuest data code page of the schema repository.	Adds two Perl hooks for all nonstateless record types: the access control hook checkCodePageMismatch and the base validation hook CharacterSetValidation.	—
	You can apply the CharacterSet Validation package with the Package Wizard and with the apply_character_set_validation_package command.	Adds a new stateless record type called _ratl_data_code_page.	
ClearCase (read-only)	Provides basic support for the Rational Base ClearCase integration.	Adds the cc_change_set and cc_vob_object record types.	Fields included in cc_change_set record type: objects
	Note that this package does *not* set up ClearQuest to use predefined ClearCase policies; they must be set up by the ClearCase administrator.	Adds the ClearCase tab to the enabled record type.	Fields included in cc_vob_object record type: Name object_oid vob_family_uuid
			Fields added to enabled record type: cc_change_set
ContentStudio	Provides support for integration with Rational Suite ContentStudio.	Adds the ContentChangeRequest record type.	Fields included in ContentChangeRequest record type: Description Headline Note_Entry Notes_Log Owner vgnAssignee vgnCMS
	Note: ContentStudio has been end-of-lifed. The ContentStudio package is merely for backward compatibility for customers who still use it.		

		vgnDueDate vgnManagementD vgnProjectPath vgnTaskName
Customer	Supports the integration of customer data with your defect- and change-tracking system.	Fields included in the Customer record type: Attachment CallTrackingID Company Description Email Fax Name Phone
	Adds a Customer stateless record type.	
	Adds reference fields for customer information to the record type you select.	Fields added to enabled record type: Customer Customer_Severity
Email (read-only)	Supports automatic e-mail notification when records are modified.	Fields included in Email_Rule record type: Actions Action_Types CC_Actioner CC_Addr_fields CC_Additional CC_Groups CC_Users Change_Fields Display_Fields Entity_Def From_Addr Include_Defect Is_Active_Rule Filter_Query Name Operator_Value
	Creates an Email_Rule stateless record type.	
	Adds a base action to the enabled record type called Send_Email_Notif. This base action runs the e-mail rule whenever any action is invoked.	

(continued)

Table 10–1   *Common ClearQuest Packages (Continued)*

Package	Description	Added or Modified	Fields
			Show_Previous
			Source_States
			Subject_Fields
			Target_States
			To_Additional
			To_Addr_Fields
			To_Groups
			To_Users
Enhancement Request	Supports an additional record type for product enhancement requests.	Adds the Enhancement Request record type.	Customer_Company
			Customer_Email
			Customer_Name
			Customer_Phone
			Customer_Priority
			Description
			Headline
			Keywords
			Owner
			Priority
			Product
			Product_Area
			Request_Type
			Submit_Date
			Submitter
			Target_Release
History (read-only)	Lets you keep a historical account of all actions taken on a record.	Adds a History tab to the enabled record type.	No fields added

Notes	Lets you keep a historical account of all notes entered on a record, according to date and user.	Adds a Notes tab to the enabled record type. Adds a base action called Init_Note_Entry in the enabled record type, which deletes the Note_Entry value.	Fields added to enabled record type: Note_Entry Notes_Log
PQC (read-only)	Provides support for integration with Rational PurifyPlus.	Adds a PQC tab to the form of the enabled record type.	Fields added to enabled record type: PQC_DiagnosticTool PQC_Executable PQC_TestCommand PQC_TestTool PQC_Stack PQC_StackID
Project	Lets you track records according to project. **Note:** This is not related to the UCM package Project concept.	Creates a Project stateless record type.	Fields included in Project record type: Name Description Fields added to enabled record type: Project
Repository (read-only)	Provides support needed for Rational RequisitePro, Rational Administrator, and Rational TeamTest.	Creates an RAProject stateless record type.	Fields included in RAProject record type: Name TT_Repo (refers to the TeamTest Repository) RA_Project_Path Fields added to enabled record type: RAProject

(continued)

Table 10-1 *Common ClearQuest Packages (Continued)*

Package	Description	Added or Modified	Fields
[S.10.1] RequisitePro (read-only)	Provides support for integration with Rational RequisitePro.	Adds the Requirement and RequirementMap stateless record types. Adds the Requirements and the ASCQIBase base actions to the enabled record type.	Fields included in Requirement record type: Name Project_Name Req_GUID Req_ID Requirement Tag Fields included in RequirementMap record type: CQBackReqListAttName CQDatabase CQDatabasePath CQDialogTitle CQEntityDefName CQHelpContextID CQModifyAction CQReqListAttName CQRepoProjectAttName HelpFileName RPAttrGUID RPHelpContextID RPProjectName RPProjectPath RPReqTypeGUID Fields added to enabled record type: Requirements_List
Resolution	Adds support for tracking how a record was resolved. **Note:** This requires you to map schema states to the state types Not_Resolved and Resolved.	Adds a Resolution tab to the enabled record type.	Fields added to enabled record type: Resolution Resolution_Statetype (read-only)

194

		Fields added to enabled record type:
TeamTest (read-only)	Provides support for integration with Rational TeamTest.	Build Company Computer Contact Custom1 (modifiable) Custom2 (modifiable) Custom3 (modifiable) Fixed_In_Build Hardware Log Log_Folder old_internal_id Operating_System Other_Environment Resolution_Description Requirement Requirement_ID Test_Case Test_Case_UID Test_Script Test_Script_ID Test_Source_UID Test_Input_List Verification_Point
	Adds Test Data and Environment tabs to the record type you specify.	Fields added to the TestInput record type:
	Adds a TestInput stateless record type.	Test_Input_Name Test_Input_ID Source_UID
UCMPolicy Scripts	Provides support for the UCM package by adding three global scripts.	Does not add any record types. —

(continued)

Table 10–1 *Common ClearQuest Packages (Continued)*

Package	Description	Added or Modified	Fields
UnifiedChange-Management (UCM) (read-only)	Provides support for the UCM process by enabling integration with Rational ClearCase 4.0 and higher; links a ClearCase Project versioned object base (VOB) with a ClearQuest user database.	Adds the UCMUtilityActivity and UCM_Project stateless record types.	Fields included in UCMUtilityActivity record type: am_statetype Description Owner Headline ucm_vob_object ucm_stream_object ucm_stream ucm_view ucm_project
		Adds UCM queries to the client workspace in Public Folders.	Fields included in UCM_Project record type: Name ucm_vob_object ucm_chk_before_deliver ucm_chk_before_work_on ucm_chk_mstr_before_dlvr ucm_cq_act_after_deliver
	Note: Using this requires the UCMPolicy Scripts package. You can also use this with the BaseCMActivity package. It also requires you to map schema states to the following state types: Waiting, Active, Ready, Complete.	Adds the ucm_base_ synchronize action to the enabled record type.	Fields added to enabled record type: am_statetype ucm_vob_object ucm_stream_object ucm_stream ucm_view ucm_project

Visual SourceSafe (read-only)	Provides support for integration with Microsoft Visual SourceSafe.	Fields added to enabled record type: VSSChangeSet
	Adds SSObject and SCSnapObject stateless record types.	Fields added in SSObject record type: CQDefects VSSCheckOutState VSSFileName VSSSpec VSSUser VSSVersion
	Adds the SourceSafe tab to the form of the enabled record type.	Fields added in SCSnapObject record type: CreatedBy CreatedOn Label SnapElements

UCM Integration

[A.10.7] The integration between ClearQuest and Unified Change Management (UCM) enables ClearQuest to display information about a UCM activity (such as its change set, its stream, and whether it is currently set in any view). It also enables policies governing when delivery of an activity in ClearCase can occur and when a record can be closed in ClearQuest. Here's a quick description of UCM from the IBM Rational website.

> Managing the ongoing process of change is important for any development team. However, the issue is further complicated as specialized, distributed teams strive to build high-quality software in less time. Rational has responded with a model that simplifies the process of change by raising the level of abstraction so development teams can focus on activities rather than individual physical changes to files. Unified Change Management (UCM) integrates asset and activity management.
>
> [T.10.1, T.10.2] UCM is delivered through an integration of Rational ClearCase®, for software asset management, and Rational ClearQuest® for defect and change tracking. UCM provides out-of-the-box workflow for automating change across the software lifecycle and across distributed multi-functional development teams.
>
> UCM helps managers reduce risk by coordinating and prioritizing the activities of developers and by ensuring that they work with the right sets of assets. Extending across the lifecycle to accommodate all project domain information—requirements, visual models, code, and test artifacts, UCM helps teams effectively "baseline" requirements together with code and test assets. The result: accelerated team development in which quality standards are met or exceeded on time and on budget.[1]

For a more extended discussion of UCM, you may also want to check out *Software Configuration Management Strategies and IBM Rational ClearCase—Second Edition* by David E. Bellagio and Tom Milligan (IBM Press, 2005).

---

1. From IBM Rational marketing information on the website, http://www-306.ibm
   .com.

At any point in a project, your ClearQuest database may contain UCM-enabled records that aren't linked to a UCM activity object. For example, a newly created record might not be linked to a UCM activity. You must explicitly complete an action (e.g., by clicking on Action → Work On) to link a UCM-enabled record to a UCM activity.

However, the opposite is not true: Each UCM activity in a project enabled for ClearQuest must be linked to a ClearQuest record. You can't create a UCM activity object without linking it to a UCM-enabled record in a ClearQuest database.

So why would you use the UCM integration? This is basically the integration of two of IBM Rational's most powerful tools. Although not a seamless integration between defect tracking and version/change control, once configured, the combination makes for a very powerful tool that helps your engineers become more productive in their day-to-day activities.

UCM Concepts

[A.10.8] To understand the integration, you need to understand both tools. The following is a brief overview of UCM concepts. This will help you to better understand the integration between UCM and ClearQuest.

Projects

The term *project* refers to a group of people working on a single development effort. This can be a product release, a subsystem that's part of a complete system, or a collection of products to form a suite.

A project contains one integration stream and several development streams (see the next subsection). This is where you—as the change management guru—must start planning. However, before you start creating projects all over the place, you need to sit down with marketing, your software development team, QA, and your technical writers to determine how you want to work together.

Streams

A *stream* can be compared to a development branch: It basically groups specific versions of elements. The key differentiator between a generic branch and a stream is the additional information stored in the stream. For example, a stream contains a baseline and a set of activities. It also contains relationships with other streams, such as a parent stream. The baseline plus the set of activities determine what versions of the elements the stream contains.

In Figure 10–5, Activity 1 and Activity 2 have been added to the stream. The baseline is defined by the versions of the elements represented by the bold circles in the diagram. The two activities have versions of elements that represent different patterns.

There are two basic types of streams: an integration stream and a development stream. The integration stream is where all of the development streams come together to be shared, as shown in Figure 10–6.

Baselines

A *baseline* represents versions of elements used to start or rebase a stream. (Developers use the rebase operation to synchronize their streams with the new, recommended team baseline.) A simplistic way of looking at baselines is to compare them to labels, the difference again being that there is additional information and relation-

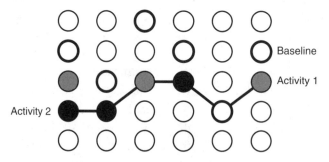

Figure 10–5   *Sample stream flow*

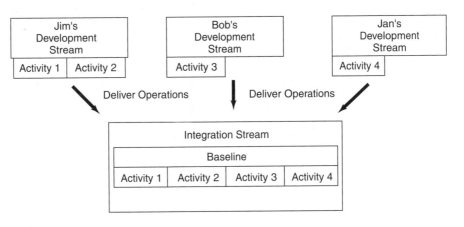

Figure 10–6   *Sample integration stream flow*

ships stored with baselines. Baselines are typically the starting point for many of your activities.

Activities

An *activity* is the basic unit of work that your team members perform. It has a headline (ID), a creator, a change set (a list of versions of elements that have been changed as a result of performing this activity), and a parent stream with which it corresponds. An activity must be created before you can create a version of an element in a ClearCase UCM project.

If you're using Rational ClearQuest, an activity is usually tied directly to a defect or enhancement. All work performed in your development stream must be done in concert with an activity.

Components

A *component* allows you to group a set of related directories and file elements and then tie them to a UCM project. A component is developed and then integrated, and then all of its parts are released together. All projects must have one or more components, and components can be shared between projects. However, a component cannot span multiple versioned object bases (VOBs), and the largest a component can be is the size of its VOB. Here are some other things to consider about components.

- Elements cannot be moved from one component to another.

- An element can exist in only one component.

- Once you create a component, you can't reorganize it into subcomponents.

Planning your components up front is extremely important. One strategy is to put any elements that will be shared with other projects into the same component or into groups of components.

ClearQuest/UCM Components and Packages

ClearQuest comes with two schemas that help in the integration of UCM: the UnifiedChangeManagement schema and the Enterprise schema. It also contains several packages used for the integration if you have your own schema that you want to enable for UCM: AMStateTypes, UCMPolicy Scripts, UnifiedChangeManagement, and BaseCMActivity. Additionally, you must set up Rational UCM to use ClearQuest integration. You can either use the schema that's been provided or add these packages to your current schema. The following sections walk through each of these approaches.

Adding the UCM Integration to Your Schema

Before you do anything here, you need to make sure that you have your schema checked out and that you have a plan. Don't follow these steps until you are sure what records you want in the UCM integration and what policies you want to enforce, and also that you have the use case model defined. Again, planning up front will save you lots of time and heartache later. See Chapters 5 and 6 on analysis and design for some pointers on designing your system and taking the necessary steps for preparation.

Okay, now that you are back from reading those chapters and you have created a plan on how to move forward, we can begin by adding the necessary packages to the schema.

Before you add the first package, make sure that you have your states and transitions defined for your records. It's much easier to add packages to an existing state net than it is to go back and add them later.

It's important that you follow the steps in order. Don't try to cut corners here. The package application to a schema is very order-dependent, and doing things out of order can cause heartburn.

The following subsections explain the steps you need to follow.

Adding the AMStateTypes Package

First, make sure that you've checked out your schema. Then go to the Package Wizard, using Package → Package Wizard within the Clear-Quest Designer. You will see the packages that you can add to your schema (Figure 10–7).

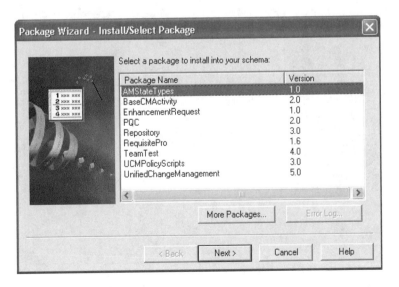

Figure 10–7 *Selecting packages*

Select the AMStateTypes package and click Next. You will see the
records in your schema. Select all of the records that need to have
AMStateTypes applied to them (Figure 10–8). This includes everything you identified in your design.

In this example, the ChangeRequest record is being applied to the
integration. If you click Next here, you will see all of the states that
are part of the ChangeRequest record. As you can see in Figure 10–9,
this allows you to map the AMStateTypes package to the states you
have in your record. These state types refer to the state types in UCM
activities (Waiting, Ready, Active, and Complete).

You need to set the state type for each state in the record. When you
have completed this for every state, you can click the Finish button.

Note that each state type has a state net of its own and that all states
assigned to a state type must follow the same transition rules as the
state type. For example, Submitted belongs to the state type Waiting.
This means that all transitions from Submitted must move to a state

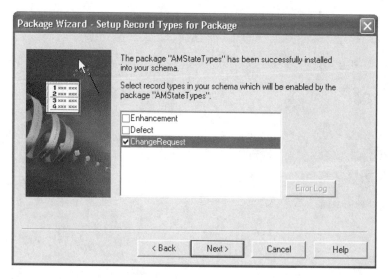

Figure 10–8   *Selecting record types*

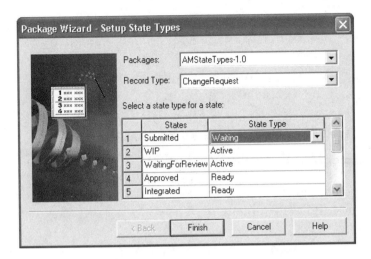

Figure 10–9 *Mapping states*

with the state type of Active or Ready. This is true for all states and state types. Figure 10–10 shows the state net for the state type and the valid transitions.

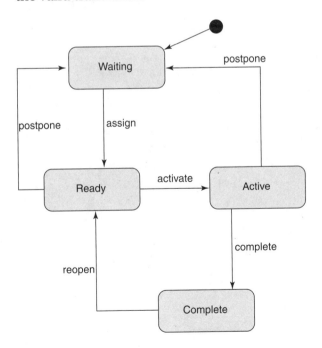

Figure 10–10 *State transitions*

To ensure that you have your state types and states set up properly, validate the schema using the File → Validate menu option.

You may find Figure 10–10 important when setting up the default actions described in the next subsection.

Setting Up the Default Actions for UCM

The State Transition Matrix associated with your schema must provide at least one path through the state type model for the Unified-ChangeManagement package, from the Waiting state type to Ready, to Active, and to Complete.

For each state in your schema (except the state mapped to the Complete state type), you must assign a default action that moves the record from that state to the next state type in the UCM state type model.

To set the default action, you need to select the state's property by right-clicking on the state and selecting the Properties item from the context menu, as shown in Figure 10–11.

A property dialog will pop up (Figure 10–12). Choose the Default Action tab, and then select one of the actions to be the default action.

You need to do this for each of your states. If you don't define a default action, you'll receive errors when you validate the schema. You must also have a default action path that flows from Waiting → Ready → Active → Complete, or a validation error will result. Once your schema validates with no errors, move to the next step.

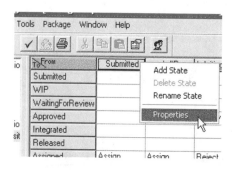

Figure 10–11   *Selecting the state's property*

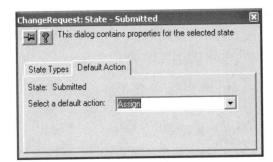

Figure 10–12   *Property dialog*

Adding the UCMPolicy Scripts Package

This package contains UCM policy scripts that will be used in the integration to change the state of records and to enforce behavior in UCM-enabled Rational ClearCase. You can see the new scripts that have been added to your schema by looking at Global Scripts within the browser (Figure 10–13).

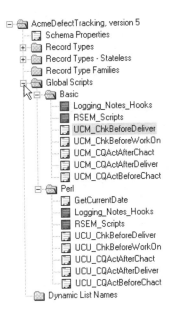

Figure 10–13   *Viewing added scripts*

There are Perl and Basic versions of these files. The names of these scripts start with UCU_<OperationName>. The name of a given operation gives you a clue as to its use.

The following list offers brief explanations of each script.

- *UCU_ChkBeforeDeliver* implements the check before delivery policy for UCM.

- *UCU_ChkBeforeWorkOn* implements the check before work on policy for UCM.

- *UCU_CQActAfterChact* implements the perform action after changing activity policy for UCM.

- *UCU_CQActAfterDeliver* implements the perform action after delivery policy for UCM.

- *UCU_CQActBeforeChact* implements the perform action before change activity policy for UCM.

A default policy is automatically written in the scripts, but you can change it using one of the provided scripting languages. If your design requires changes to these policies, this is where you would make the changes.

Adding the UnifiedChangeManagement (UCM) Package

Now you need to add the UnifiedChangeManagement package to your schema. This contains more state types, fields, and records specific to UCM. To do this, go to the Package → Package Wizard menu item to open the Package Wizard (Figure 10–14).

Then select the UnifiedChangeManagement package and click Next. ClearQuest will present the record types against which you could apply the package. In our example in Figure 10–15, we have selected the ChangeRequest record. Again, look at your design to see what records you want to be part of the UCM integration.

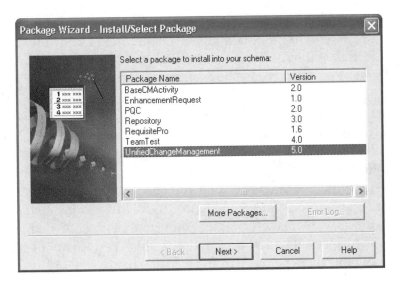

Figure 10–14   *Selecting a package to install*

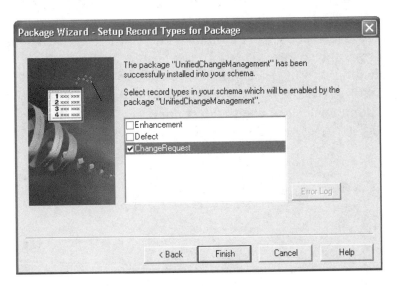

Figure 10–15   *Selecting the ChangeRequest record*

The records you choose to apply to this package must have, at minimum, values in the Headline and Owner fields. They must also have a Modify action defined, and they cannot have a WorkOn action defined. You'll receive an error if either of these conditions doesn't hold true.

Click Finish when you're done applying records to your package. You will see a new record name: UCMUtilityActivity. This record stores information about the UCM activity. You will also see additional fields added to the record that you chose to be enabled with this package. As you can see in Figure 10–16, these fields include ucm_vob_object, ucm_stream_object, ucm_stream, ucm_view, and ucm_project. If you don't see these fields, then ClearQuest didn't apply the given package to the record you are viewing.

Additionally, two actions are added to the record: WorkOn and ucm_base_synchronize. These help with the integration. Additional scripts are added at this time, as well.

Adding the BaseCMActivity Package

This package is optional, and we don't recommend using it unless you don't already have a record to handle basic change management activities. It adds a record named BaseCMActivity with fields, states, forms, and so forth. This could be a good starting point if you are creating your own schema from scratch that you want to be UCM-enabled. To do this, go to the Package → Package Wizard menu item. A popup will allow you to select the BaseCMActivity package (Figure 10–17).

am_statetype	STATETYPE	
Headline	SHORT_STRING	
Owner	REFERENCE	
ucm_vob_object	SHORT_STRING	
ucm_stream_object	SHORT_STRING	
ucm_stream	SHORT_STRING	BASIC,PERL
ucm_view	SHORT_STRING	BASIC,PERL
ucm_project	REFERENCE	BASIC,PERL

Figure 10–16 *Applied fields*

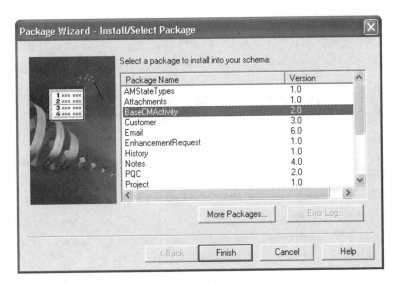

Figure 10–17   *Selecting the BaseCMActivity package*

Now click Finish. ClearQuest will add the new record to your schema. The record will have the following fields:

- Owner

- Description

- Headline

The state net for the record will have the basic steps defined for the UCM integration. The State Transition Matrix will look like Figure 10–18.

To\From	Submitted	Ready	Active	Complete
Submitted		Postpone	Postpone	
Ready	Assign			Re_open
Active		Activate		
Complete			Complete	

Figure 10–18   *State net record*

Some basic forms are also available for Submit and Modify actions. They look basically the same. Figure 10–19 is an example of how these forms look.

Now that ClearQuest is set up, you will need to set up UCM-enabled Rational ClearCase to talk with ClearQuest. For that, keep reading.

Setting Up IBM Rational UCM for ClearQuest Integration

[A.10.9] In order to have UCM and ClearQuest integrated, you must have a UCM project that has been enabled for ClearQuest. To do this, you need to make sure that you have ClearCase and ClearQuest installed on the same system. Once this is completed, you can enable the integration using the Project Explorer. Here are the steps.

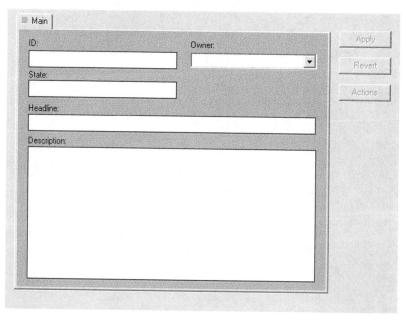

Figure 10–19 *Basic form*

1. [S.10.2] Right-click on the project shortcut in the UCM Explorer, then click on Properties.

2. Click on the ClearQuest tab, and then select the Project Is ClearQuest-Enabled check box. Then, select the user database that you want to link to the project. The first time you enable a project to ClearQuest, it will prompt you for a ClearQuest login and the database to which the project will be connected.

3. Select the UCM policies that you want the project to enforce, and then click OK.

[A.10.10] Now you are ready to start using the integration. A great resource for the UCM/ClearQuest integration can be found in the ClearCase documentation in the *Managing Software Projects* manual.

Developing Your Own Integration

[S.10.3] Before starting your integration with other tools, you need to look closely at your use case analysis and design. Look for the software actors in your system to see what kinds of communication channels need to be established between the two applications. Remember that these were only predictions; you are allowed to change your design as needed. Sometimes you can get stuck on your original design, and the implementation becomes unattainable. So, just remember to stay flexible throughout your deployment, and be prepared to make changes.

Tool integration requires an in-depth knowledge of the tools that you're integrating. Most tools have some kind of API or import/export mechanism. Keep in mind that the integrations need to run on the client side of ClearQuest, and therefore the API to the integrated system needs to exist on the same platform and/or system. Of course, transport mechanisms can be used to make things more platform-independent, such as e-mail or XML, but both systems must understand them. Realizing the limitations of tool integration is the first step to making a useful integration.

You also need to realize that the tools you will be integrating will have an overlap of information. The key is to limit this overlap as much as possible and also to determine which tool has the "golden" information (the information that will be considered correct all the time). All of the others, then, are copies of the information; they can be reconstituted as needed.

Once you have determined where your golden information is and what kind of integration APIs you can use, you should look next at how the information will be synchronized or obtained from the external tool or from ClearQuest. There's a great article by Mike Exum on ClearQuest integration at IBM developerWorks,[2] in which he describes integrations as inbound, outbound, or a combination of both. The following subsections offer some definitions to help you understand these concepts.

Outbound Integration

With outbound integrations, ClearQuest will push information to an external tool for integration. It's natural to use a ClearQuest hook to interact with the other application. However, this is not as easy or straightforward as you might think.

First, you need to realize where the hook will be executed and whether the other application's API can be accessed from the same machine. Hooks are run on the ClearQuest client machine—both UNIX and Windows—and on the web server in the case of the web client. So, you need to make sure that your integrated application is available on these hosts. (Keep in mind that this may require installation of the application on these hosts.)

Second, you need to decide where the hook should be placed. When the hook runs, should it be run by the user, should it be automatically run when a record changes state, or should it be run periodi-

---

2. "A Primer on ClearQuest Integrations," http://www.ibm.com/developerworks/rational/library/1051.html.

cally? These decisions can make your integration easier or harder. For example, if you choose to send information to an application and that takes a long time, then attaching the hook to a change state of a record will probably be painful for the user.

Finally, you need to consider security. Do the applications require different users and user authentication? Does the authentication require user interaction? What other restrictions and/or security rules might prevent some or all of the actions needed by the integration?

Inbound Integration

Inbound integrations are those in which ClearQuest will receive information from another application. Basically, the issues are very similar to those surrounding outbound integration, but the roles are reversed. ClearQuest has a COM interface that makes several languages available to the integrator, including Visual Basic, VBScript, Visual C++, and Perl. ClearQuest also comes with its own customized version of Perl, which you can use directly. For more information on the ClearQuest API, see the ClearQuest API guide. There are several different aspects to the API, but we can't cover the API in this book. There is also a command-line interface for support on UNIX and Linux clients.

[A.10.11] Again, you need to consider the same things as with outbound integration. ClearQuest does offer several different options for its API, but you should remember that you will need to install the ClearQuest client on all of the machines that need to run the integration.

Data Translation

Many times, tools have different names for the same concept, or at least different values for the same concept. A typical example of this is when ClearQuest uses one name and set of values to represent the severity of a defect while an integrated CRM system uses a completely different name with different values. Table 10–2 is an example

Table 10–2 *CRM Translation Table*

CRM Severity	ClearQuest Defect Severity
Fatal	1
Critical	2
Guarded	3
Annoyance	4
Suggestion	5

of a translation table between the defect severity values in a CRM system and in the ClearQuest Defect record.

Therefore, in your integration, you would need to convert from the CRM severity value to the ClearQuest defect severity value, and vice versa.

developerWorks Links

A.10.1   http://www-128.ibm.com/developerworks/rational/library/1051.html

A.10.2   http://www-128.ibm.com/developerworks/rational/library/5211.html

A.10.3   http://www-128.ibm.com/developerworks/rational/library/131.html

A.10.4   http://www-128.ibm.com/developerworks/rational/library/3792.html

A.10.5   http://www-128.ibm.com/developerworks/rational/library/271.html

A.10.6   http://www-128.ibm.com/developerworks/rational/library/sep05/lee/

S.10.1   http://www-128.ibm.com/developerworks/rational/library/5080.html

A.10.7   http://www-128.ibm.com/developerworks/rational/library/74.html

T.10.1   http://www-128.ibm.com/developerworks/rational/library/4203.html

T.10.2   http://www-128.ibm.com/developerworks/edu/i-dw-r-automatesrm-i.html

A.10.8   http://www-128.ibm.com/developerworks/rational/library/3316.html

A.10.9   http://www-128.ibm.com/developerworks/rational/library/1763.html

S.10.2   http://www-128.ibm.com/developerworks/rational/library/4433.html

A.10.10   http://www-128.ibm.com/developerworks/rational/library/5772.html

S.10.3   http://www-128.ibm.com/developerworks/rational/library/3900.html

A.10.11   http://www-128.ibm.com/developerworks/rational/library/4125.html

11

Deployment and Administration

[A.11.1–A.11.4] At some point in every project, you must actually put your plan into action and subsequently manage the results of your implementation. As with the planning and design phases, it is always good to know the options and the various components of your deployment and ongoing administration before moving forward. Understanding all of the different pieces will help you avoid snags in your deployment—and, more importantly, to manage your user expectations better.

Knowing Your Databases

One of the fundamentals of effective ClearQuest usage involves managing your databases. Understanding the different types of databases used in ClearQuest and the nuances of working with each of the major database vendors will help you in your planning efforts.

There are three basic types of databases.

1. **User database**: While there is not really a separate user database—user data is stored in the schema repository and replicated in the production/test database—it is important to identify this piece as it does usually exist separately. It contains all of the users and groups with permissions and access rights for ClearQuest. You'll use the ClearQuest User Administration tool to manage this database.

2. **Schema repository**: This contains the schemas for the production databases; you manage it using the ClearQuest Designer tool. The database keeps versions of all of the schemas in use.

3. **Production database**: This contains the actual data for production use, including all of the items defined by the records in the schema repository. This database is populated and used by all ClearQuest users.

In addition to these databases, we also recommend with any deployment the use of test, user acceptance testing, and training databases, as required for your organization.

Establishing Connections

ClearQuest allows you to create collections, or groupings, of the three basic databases. Each grouping is referred to as a *connection.*

You create a connection by using the ClearQuest Maintenance Tool. In order to use ClearQuest, you must have at least one connection created. When you install ClearQuest for the first time, it will create a connection for you by default.

Of course, depending on your ClearQuest architecture and company needs, you can have more than one connection per ClearQuest install. Why would you need to create multiple connections? Well, for one, the connections can use different back-end databases to store the three databases defined earlier. Again, it all depends on what database vendors your company might be using at various sites; ClearQuest provides some flexibility in how you architect your solution.

[A.11.5] Let's walk through the creation of a connection using the ClearQuest Maintenance Tool. First, open the ClearQuest Maintenance Tool. You will see the dialog box shown in Figure 11–1.

If you have not added connections beyond the default, you will see the one connection, as shown in the figure. If you've already added more than one connection, they should all show up here.

You can create two basic types of artifacts using this dialog: connections and schema repositories. (The latter includes connections.)

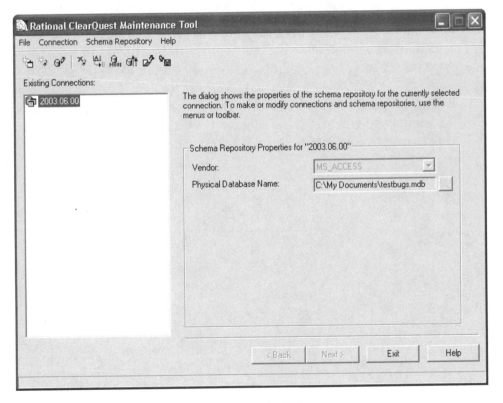

Figure 11–1   *ClearQuest Maintenance Tool window*

Connections are basically references to a schema repository. If you create a connection using the Connection → Create menu item, ClearQuest will prompt you for a database in which to connect (Figure 11–2).

You must enter a valid schema repository for the connection. If you don't, you'll receive an error.

Creating a schema repository does a couple of things: It will create a new schema repository, and it will also connect the repository to a database and create a connection containing all of the necessary information. To do this, go to the menu item Schema Repository → Create, which will bring up the window shown in Figure 11–3.

This will result in a new schema repository database.

Now click the Next button and choose which code page you want to use. In most cases, the default settings should meet your needs. Click Next once again. A new dialog will appear (Figure 11–4).

The ClearQuest Wizard will set up a sample database and populate it with some data based on the schema that you choose. Of course, you don't have to create this database at this time. In fact, if you're plan-

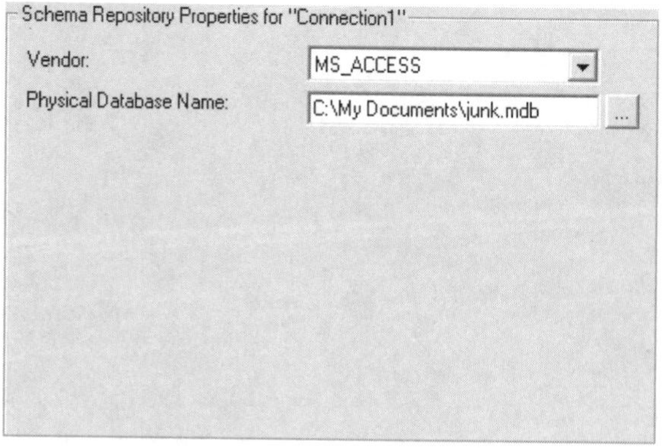

Figure 11–2   *Creating a connection*

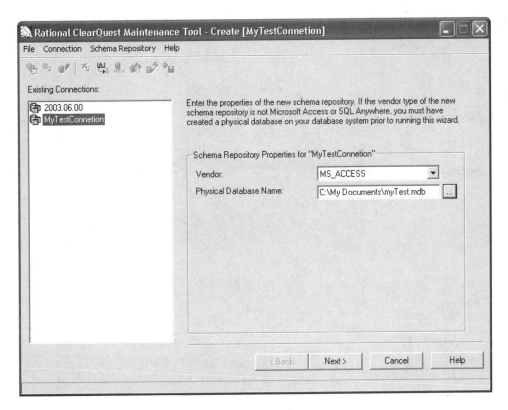

Figure 11–3 *Creating a schema repository*

ning to create your own schema, we suggest avoiding the step at this time. You can always create a sample database later by using Clear-Quest Designer. If you do decide to create the sample database now, ClearQuest will prompt you for the database information after you click the Next button.

Creating User Databases

In order to use the schemas to create production databases, you will need to create a user database. This database contains user and group information for all of the databases, including access and permissions settings.

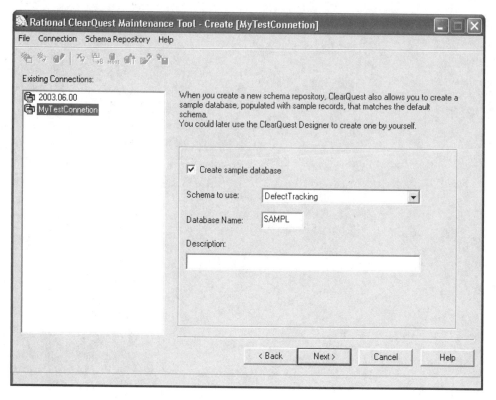

Figure 11–4   *Creating a sample database*

To create a user database, open the ClearQuest Designer tool. You will probably see the Open Schema dialog box. Just click Cancel. Now you can create a user database by using the Database → New Database menu item, which opens the window shown in Figure 11–5.

The logical database name is limited to five characters, so be creative.

Now, click the Next button. ClearQuest will prompt you with database configuration options for each of the various vendors that it supports. In the example shown in Figure 11–6, we have selected MS_ACCESS for simplicity.

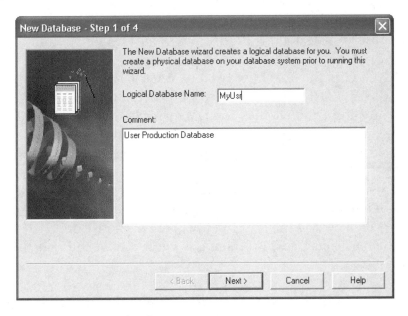

Figure 11–5 *Creating a user database*

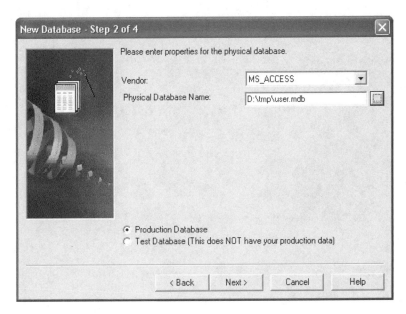

Figure 11–6 *Selecting the physical database*

Because we're going to create a production database, not a test database, we selected the Production Database radio button.

Now click the Next button again. You will see timing information for the database. Just leave these at the default settings at this time. (See Creating New Schemas and Databases in Chapter 7 for a discussion of timing information.) Click the Next button again. The dialog shown in Figure 11–7 will appear.

Select the schema with which the user database will be associated. Remember: This should be the same as the schema you will use in production. In this case, we are going to choose the AcmeDefectTracking schema, so we'll select it and click the Finish button.

You now have a user database to which you can add users. Pat yourself on the back.

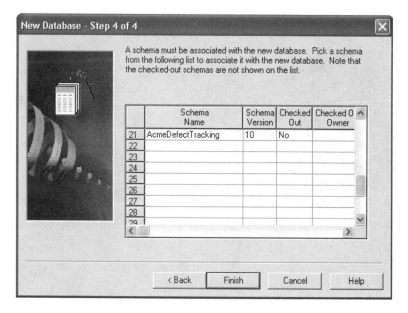

Figure 11–7   *Associating a schema with the database*

Database Backups

Redundancy is always a good rule of thumb. It's important to use the backup tools available with your chosen database. Many commercial databases have a backup scheme that is easy to use. Also, it is critical that you back up all of the ClearQuest databases at the same time. This includes the user, schema, and any working databases. If you don't, you run the risk of your databases getting out of sync, which will make ClearQuest unusable. So, you need to make sure that you establish—and stick to—some kind of backup procedure.

Web Client or No Web Client?

You need to decide how your users are going to access the ClearQuest client. You have basically two options: ClearQuest client or ClearQuest Web client.

The web client is a good option if you have individuals who travel a lot or are often remote and prefer to access your system through the web. If you don't think you will need the web interface now, think about the future growth and development of your team and projects; many organizations at least include the web interface in their planning, which allows them to provide some flexibility to their users later.

If you decide to go with the web client, you need to decide which web installation works best for your deployment. Four installation configurations are recommended by the ClearQuest manual for the web client: simple, extended, optimized, and hybrid. In all of these cases, you will need two components: the ClearQuest Web component and the ClearQuest Server component.

Simple Configuration

The simple configuration is the easiest to install and maintain. Most small to mid-size organizations stick with the simple configuration and typically use a Windows server as the single machine on which everything is installed. Figure 11–8 illustrates how this selection is configured.

Extended Configuration

The extended configuration, as shown in Figure 11–9, uses another computer to handle failover and load balancing.

This configuration works best for larger organizations where the installation is used heavily. It requires more setup and management, so before moving to this type of installation, make sure you understand the time and effort involved in maintaining this configuration.

Optimized Configuration

The optimized configuration, as shown in Figure 11–10, involves each component running on its own machine.

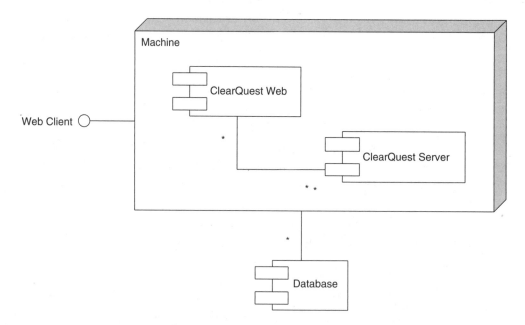

Figure 11–8   *Simple web configuration*

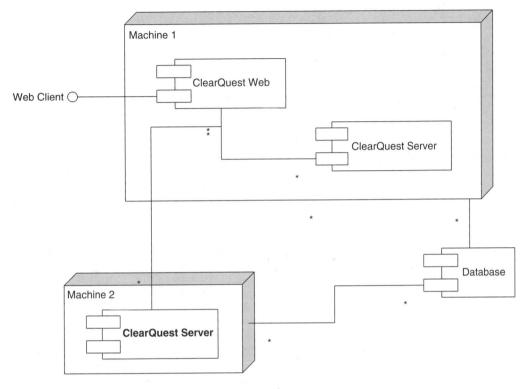

Figure 11–9   *Extended web configuration*

This configuration is for very large organizations or organizations that have performance issues with the web client. Again, having more machines means more installation setup and maintenance.

Hybrid Configuration

The hybrid configuration involves using both UNIX and Windows in your configurations. The most likely combination is UNIX for the client and Windows for the servers.

Installation Steps

Once you have chosen what configuration you want to use, you now need to figure out what web servers, databases, operating systems, and other tools you might integrate are supported by ClearQuest.

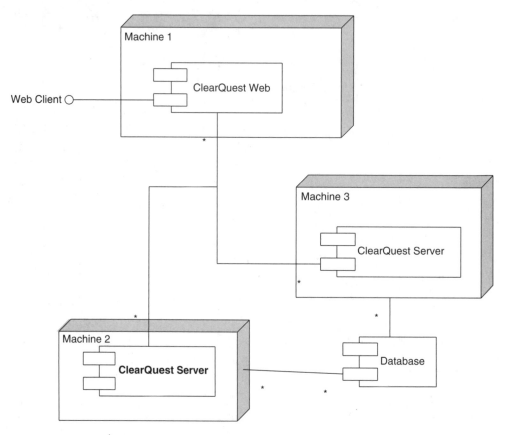

Figure 11–10   *Optimized web configuration*

The best place to find this information is in the *ClearQuest Web Installation* guide.

We don't include this information here because it can change too often to be practical, and you're better served by getting the latest information on the IBM Rational website. Chapter 10 provides some links that you may find useful. Make sure that you have specifications for all of the required components and for both Windows and UNIX configurations, as necessary.

Now that you have confirmed the configuration and versioned components requirements, you can proceed with the following preinstallation steps.

1. *Install a web browser.* You need to have both JavaScript and plug-ins enabled on the browser.

2. *Install ClearQuest Administration tools.* This is part of the main ClearQuest installation.

3. *Install ClearQuest MultiSite Administration tools.* If you are working with a multisite installation, you must install this; if not, don't install this toolset.

4. *Install database client software.* If your selected database requires specific client software, then it must be installed so the ClearQuest server can access the database.

After the preinstalls are done, you can install ClearQuest Web from either the web or from CD. Remember that you will need to install the software as the administrator, and make sure you select the ClearQuest Web components. Follow the installation, as it will guide you through the setup process step-by-step.

Postinstallation Steps

There are several postinstallation steps; which ones you take depends on the platform and database type. However, the basic steps are the same for both UNIX and Windows. For details on these steps, see the *ClearQuest Web Installation* guide. In the meantime, prepare by doing the following.

- If you are using a DB2 database, you must create a database alias on the ClearQuest Web and ClearQuest server machines.

- You must set up a schema repository and user databases (see Chapter 7).

- If you are going to support a language other than English, you need to set up the code pages for the ClearQuest installation.

- You need to create a connection on the ClearQuest Server host to the databases. You can do this with the ClearQuest Maintenance Tool. (If you have everything on one machine, you can probably skip this step.)

- If you are using multihost configuration, you must modify the jtl.properties files on the hosts where the ClearQuest Web application and ClearQuest servers are installed. For more information on modifying this, see the *ClearQuest Web Interface* manual.

Validating Your Web Setup

After you have completed the installation of ClearQuest for the web, you should make sure that things are working. It is very easy to check the installation; simply type http:/<host>/cqweb (where <host> is the name of the host where you installed the ClearQuest Web application).

ClearQuest should prompt you to type in a user name and password. Use the ClearQuest user name and password. It will then prompt you for a database connection. Select the database connection that you set up in the previous steps. Next, the system will ask you to indicate the database with which to connect. Select any of the databases that have already been set up. Now you should have the complete ClearQuest Web client in your browser, with the same general functionality in the web as in the native ClearQuest client.

One quick best practice for this stage: It's always a good idea, if you're using the ClearQuest Web client, for your users to validate all of your schemas. Using your test databases, validate the schema using both the ClearQuest Web server and the ClearQuest client applications. It never hurts to double-check.

Training

Once you have set up your installation and defined all of your schemas, you can tell your boss that you now have plenty of time on your hands and can move to the next project. Not really. We can joke about this, and yet—unfortunately—far too often, this is exactly what happens at this stage.

One of the key elements missing in these deployments is good training. Without proper training, your newly minted ClearQuest deployment will never be properly embraced by your users, and it will not have full management support.

Your next comment to your boss *should* be that it's now time to train all of the users on how to navigate and use the tool. Of course, the boss's knee-jerk reaction will be to call IBM Rational and arrange for some training. However, you should really think through your training needs before making any decisions. First off, you don't want to waste your money on ClearQuest training for all of the users of your system. Why? It's your system, not IBM's. You designed the schema, you know the workflow, and you know how you want people to use it. Why would you hand that training over to a stranger?

There are plenty of training materials available on the web, but the most critical aspect of your training is not how to use the tool itself— the users will pick up on that quickly enough. The most critical part is to walk through the workflow and handoffs between teams.

Remember to keep the training focused on what you want the users to accomplish with the tool. If you don't want the users to create their own schemas and databases, then don't teach them how to do those things. Instead, teach them how to use the records, actions, and states that you designed for them to use. Teach them how to use reports, how to create their own reports, and how to give you feedback on making ClearQuest better.

If you are using one of the standard schemas, the ClearQuest documentation is a good place to start developing your training materials. You also need to make sure that you include any other tools with which the users will be interacting during training. For example, if you are using the ClearQuest UCM integration, you should include some of the UCM concepts in your training.

Remember to tailor your training to the different types and levels of users. Some of your software engineers may want to jump quickly into the advanced topics; you should create a small training session for those power users. You may have some other developers who don't need such in-depth training; you can show them only the minimum necessary for them to report their bugs and enhancements.

Once you've decided on your best training approach, go back to your boss and let him or her know what your plans are and how you can save the company money on training. Illustrate how the entire software development team will be more productive if the effort is driven internally. Then ask for that 30 percent raise that you know you deserve. Good luck.

Legacy Systems and Data Migration

[A.11.6] In an ideal world, you start a new software development project with all of the change management tools we've talked about already in place. Rumor has it that one person out there has had this luxury—just once. Even when all the tools are in place at the beginning, however, there will inevitably be changes later. So keep your head in reality! Most deployments typically involve some kind of legacy defect-tracking system that the company has been using for 10 years, which may or may not have been developed by the CEO's 16-year-old son. Whatever its origin, everyone has become accustomed to its many nuances and pitfalls, and countless scripts have been written to help the team move around the system.

Now you have designed and implemented a new state-of-the-art defect-tracking system, using ClearQuest with integrations into all of the latest and greatest tools. You have already sold management on moving to the new system, with promises of productivity increases of 40 percent over the next year. So how do you make this change happen without causing any major problems with current development? This is a difficult question to answer. You might consider a couple of approaches, each with its own pros and cons. We explore these approaches in the following subsections.

Burning the Bridges

This approach involves putting a date on a calendar and telling everyone that the new system is going online on this date and that all of the old data will be available only in the old system—which will be shut down soon. Only new data can be entered into the system.

This approach can be used for groups that are starting new versions of their products and will no longer support old versions. This is good for new products or for groups working as skunk works. The downside is that you will be losing all of the historical data—unless you keep the old system available, port the data over to a reporting tool, or just make it available in database form. Of course, this can make users very frustrated if they are constantly moving back and forth between the two systems or have to dig up data on Access every time they need to reference something. The upside is you don't have to do as much work. You can just focus on the new implementation and let the old system die a miserable death.

Phased Approach

A modification to the previous strategy involves including a stage or specific date in which data from the old system will be migrated to the new system. At that point, everyone will begin using the new system. The big question is: What data will you migrate?

Some will argue that all that's needed is to migrate just the open defects from the old system, with all of the historical data left on the old system. This is a valid approach, but you might as well go with the dual-system solution (see the next subsection), as people will still have to go back and forth between the two systems. So there is very little gain if you don't, at some planned point in time, cut off the old tool.

Migrating all of the data is the best option, but it can take a long time. So, you need to make a decision. Everyone wants all of the old historical data, but this is sometimes just not reasonable. Instead, put a date on the calendar and let everyone know that data will not be available on the old system after that time.

The downside of this option is that it takes lots of planning and coding from your perspective. You need to be able to migrate all of the data, plan around everyone's product releases, and try to keep management from being scared that everything is going to be accidentally erased.

To mitigate risk and allay some of the fears that are likely to be floating around, you can run your deployment in what people call "shadow mode." The best approach for shadow mode is to select a small group on which to try out the new system you've developed, preferably on a new project. This will help you work out any bugs or use model issues before you go live.

At the same time, you'll need to work on the migration script to move data from the old system to the new system. You should test this script several times to make sure that everything is working; this will give you some inkling of how long the complete migration will take. If your conversion is going to take longer than management is comfortable with, due to users not being able to access any data, then you'll need to consider using a phased approach. Of course, if you can avoid a phased approach, you will be in better shape. Phased migration of data can be very problematic. It's better to make the time to switch everything at once.

Finally, stock up on plenty of soda and pizza because you will be spending some late nights and weekends making sure that everything is working properly.

Dual-System Solution

We would prefer not to even mention this method, but it is often the reality of how organizations move forward with new tools. It shows that your company may not have bought into your vision for configuration management or your role as change agent. When you decide to not make waves and to design a system that will use the same interface the users are used to using (try saying that ten times quickly), opting to just replace the back end, you will run into problems and, ultimately, cause more work for yourself.

Maybe your current interface is sufficient and your company is just used to it, so why change things, right? With ClearQuest, you can make the forms look basically like anything you have now—except with more up-to-date technology and integrations on the back end. So, the status quo is a lame excuse for not improving your change management systems.

You may be thinking, "But the engineers have written all of these custom scripts to increase their productivity, and they don't want to change all of them." If you did a proper analysis, you will have already identified their use models and incorporated them into your design. If not, then you need to ask the engineers why they are still doing things the way you already determined was not efficient. Remember, your job is to help everyone do his or her work more effectively.

[A.11.7] The last reason to keep things the same is you are afraid of ruffling the CEO, whose teenage son, if you recall, wrote the original system. Well, this is a valid concern—of course, you don't want to offend your CEO. Well, actually, you do. Remember that you already received executive buy-in to do this project, so stand up for what you believe in. And make sure that you are actually improving things, not just acquiescing to please the ego of someone in upper management. Politics do play an important role in making changes, but if you do your homework and show how the new system will increase productivity—and how applying more bandages to the old system will continue to perpetuate the same ineffective mode of operation—you'll find that people will buy into and support the new deployment very quickly.

developerWorks Links

A.11.1   http://www-128.ibm.com/developerworks/rational/
library/5211.html

A.11.2   http://www-128.ibm.com/developerworks/rational/
library/4094.html

A.11.3   http://www-128.ibm.com/developerworks/rational/
library/4508.html

A.11.4   http://www-128.ibm.com/developerworks/rational/
library/5503.html

A.11.5   http://www-128.ibm.com/developerworks/rational/
library/nov04/courtney/

A.11.6   http://www-128.ibm.com/developerworks/rational/
library/05/r-3092/

A.11.7   http://www-128.ibm.com/developerworks/rational/
library/3943.html

12

Multisite Development

[A.12.1] Development projects are being increasingly spread across geographical boundaries, with most teams experiencing some degree of "virtual team" or multisite development. Components may be outsourced; developers may log on from home; partners or other engineering teams could have been added to the project through acquisition. Taking all of this into account, when is it appropriate to use ClearQuest MultiSite?

Increasingly, development teams span multiple, geographically dispersed sites, work on different platforms, and encompass a variety of different roles. Rational ClearQuest MultiSite, an optional add-on for Rational ClearQuest, provides full ClearQuest functionality to all team members, regardless of location. Based on the proven technology in Rational ClearCase MultiSite, Rational ClearQuest MultiSite provides the safest, most reliable means to share change request information with geographically dispersed team members. ClearQuest MultiSite helps distributed project teams efficiently work together by providing local access to replicated defect and change tracking data and by enabling automatic synchronization of that data at any time. When combined with Rational ClearCase and ClearCase MultiSite, it provides a complete, distributed software configuration management solution.[1]

[S.12.1] Clearly, the timing for moving to ClearQuest MultiSite depends on your deployment model and the needs of your team. Whether your plans include an immediate multisite deployment or a long-term strategy to move over once your organization demands the move, it is critical that you understand what is involved so that you can plan appropriately.

ClearQuest MultiSite Concepts

[S.12.2] ClearQuest has different concepts that are unique to its multisite implementation. These concepts give ClearQuest flexibility to design your configuration to work with other tools in an integrated manner.

[A.12.2] Remember that a ClearQuest installation consists of a set of databases. When you are exploring a multisite deployment, you must make sure that all of the databases in the set are replicated and transported together. Sending the schema repository together with the user databases allows you to move the schema around, applying it to any user database. If just the user database is replicated, the data cannot be accessed, and no actual data about your product development will be available at remote sites. In other words, the schema repository is required to access the user database data.

Table 12–1 explains some terminology used in the sometimes-confusing world of multisite development.

---

1. http://www.infosgroup.com/paginas/v4/publico/whitepaper/rational/Rational_ClearQuest.pdf.

Table 12–1   *ClearQuest MultiSite Terminology*

Term	Definition
Replica	A copy of a user database or a schema repository. To refer to a replica, use the site name and family name (see below).
Family	All of the replicas of a specific user database or all of the replicas of a specific schema repository. The family name of a user database replica is the database name of the originating database. The family name of a schema repository is always MASTR.
Site	A schema repository replica and its user database replicas.
Clan	All of the replicas of a schema repository and all of the replicas of the associated user databases. Replicas originating from the same database set use the same clan name, which is specified when the database set is activated.
Host (also synchronization server)	The LAN name or IP address of the network node that handles packets for a site. This host must have the ClearQuest shipping server installed on it.

Clans, Families, and Sites

These three terms—clans, families, and sites—describe different aspects of multisite development.

At first glance, it might appear that a clan consists of all of the families, but it is not obvious where the site fits in. In reality, the *clan* is defined as all of the replicas of all of the data, across all locations. A *family* consists of all of the replicas of a *single* database across all sites. A *site* consists of all of the databases required to run ClearQuest (the schema repository and the appropriate user databases).

To help you understand these terms, let's use a real-life example. Assume we have a development team spread over three locations: Hong Kong, Boston, and Paris. Let's also assume that there are two user databases, named SRC and DOC. Of course, there must also be a schema repository; by default, this has the name MASTR.

Figure 12–1 shows the clan that represents the multisite installation.

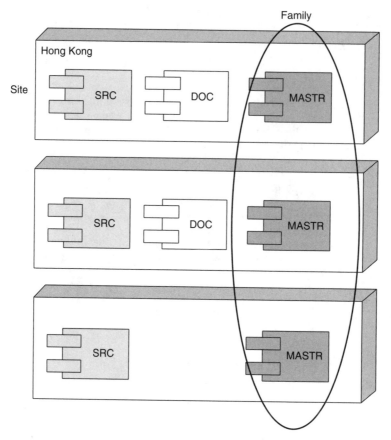

Figure 12–1   *Multisite installation clan*

As you can see, there are three sites, but not all of the sites have replicas of all of the databases. There are three families: SRC, DOC, and MASTR. Notice in the DOC family that there are only two database replicas, while the others have three. In this example, the Paris location does not need to have access to the DOC user database.

Schema Repository Types

The term *replica* has appeared a few times without any discussion. So let's define it now.

A *replica* is a copy of a database, with information about the database location(s) and a timestamp of when the copies were made. In order to keep the sites synced, information about the replicas is stored at each location where the database resides. Each replica is recorded in a table in the schema repository database. This table, which is also replicated, includes critical information about the replica, such as the name of the associated synchronization server. In addition, each schema repository database contains information about how to connect to each database in its database set. This information is not replicated.

To facilitate the multisite synchronization, most information stored in ClearQuest databases is replicated, except for checked-out copies of schemas and the schemas of user databases. (Local administrators must choose when to upgrade user databases.)

Synchronization

Synchronization is the act of making sure that copies of the database have the same information. As just mentioned, information about each replica is stored in a table in the schema repository. Because of this, information about the replicas is stored in the database and is constantly changing. The replicas tend to diverge and typically will never be in sync.

To keep things in sync, a replica will send information to one or more other replicas in the family. Updating a user database replica may change both its database and its schema repository to reflect the activity that has taken place in one or more other replicas.

Information is exported from one site to other sites in packets. A *packet* contains all of the information needed to create or update a replica. Since export and transport mechanisms can be varied and are fundamentally unreliable, logical packets can be broken into smaller physical packets as well.

Packets are created using one of two ClearQuest commands, mkreplica or syncreplica, invoked with the -export option. The packet is then sent to the remote location. It is processed on the other side by the ClearQuest mkreplica or syncreplica commands with the -import option. This basically imports the records, tables, and data into the remote site databases, as shown in Figure 12–2.

In this example, Hong Kong calls syncreplica -export, and then, using e-mail, the ClearQuest shipping server. The company may even mail CDs from Hong Kong to Boston; the point is to deliver the data. Once the packets get to Boston from Hong Kong (it doesn't matter how or how long it takes), syncreplica -import is called on the package, and the Boston site's DEV database is updated.

Synchronization can happen at the family level. This means that you can sync a given family at a different interval than another database's family. A good example of this might be syncing a DEV family every hour and syncing a DOC family once a day, depending on how often things are changing in the environment.

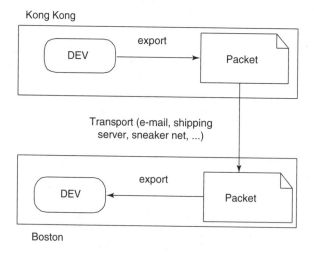

Figure 12–2 *Information transported by packet*

Mastership

[S.12.3, S.12.4] Changes at the multiple sites are done independently of each other. Because of this restriction, there is a healthy chance that you may encounter conflicts. For example, two people or two software applications could update the same object at the same time.

[T.12.1] For this reason, the concept of mastership has been defined. Essentially, *mastership* determines which site owns and can change an object. The mastership can be transferred from one site to another site, as needed.

Each of the following objects has a mastership replica:

- Records
- Users and groups
- Workspace items (queries, reports, charts, and folders)
- Schema repositories

For user database records, mastership information is stored as a field value in a record. Users can change the value of the Mastership field to transfer mastership to another replica. Mastership of the record is sent to the new master replica during the next synchronization. For all other database objects, an administrator must change the mastership.

It's very important to teach your users the mastership concept; it will fundamentally change the way they work. Here's a common team workflow example: A team in Hong Kong is testing a product and enters a defect against the product into ClearQuest. The mastership of the defect is in Hong Kong, which means that no other site can change the object. If the team fixing the defect is in Boston, then the team in Hong Kong must set the mastership to Boston so they can make changes to the defect record within the database.

If you have your sites set up to handle specific aspects of development (e.g., Boston owns the user interface, while Paris owns the back-end transaction portion of your solution), you can design your mastership policy for automation with scripting hooks. In the previous example, if all of the testing takes place in Hong Kong but all of the development is done in Boston, then a submission hook can be written to transfer mastership to the Boston development team automatically.

Designing your mastership migration can be just as important as the records themselves. If the tool gets in the way of users doing effective work, then the users will revolt and find ways around the tool.

Resolving Conflicts

Sometimes two objects, such as user objects, are created at different sites but with the same name. A good way to prevent this from happening is to create and enforce a naming convention at each site and for each replica family. For example, for site-specific objects (e.g., workspace objects and stateless records), you can include the site name in the name of the object. For objects used in multiple sites, choose a single site where that type of object is created and then replicated to all of the other sites.

Internally, ClearQuest ensures that some records and workspace names are unique.

- For record types that use states, ClearQuest uses database ID numbers to ensure uniqueness.

- For stateless record types (including users and groups), ClearQuest uses unique keys and stores the name of the originating site or keysite.

- For workspace items, ClearQuest stores the name of the originating site or keysite and the name of the workspace item.

So, if ClearQuest guarantees uniqueness of all of the objects in the database, why should you care if you have two objects with the same name? The confusion comes when you try to access the object from ClearQuest Web or from a different site. You will get only one of the objects, and in the case of ClearQuest Web, it can be indeterminate.

A worst-case scenario is that you make changes to an object on one site, and then you don't see the changes at another site after syncing your systems. Your users will then complain that your defect-tracking system doesn't work, and they'll refuse to use it because they think it's losing information.

A simple example of this is creating defects with the same title. Why would someone do this? *Because it can be done.* Or you may have two teams at different locations doing similar work. At first, your users will complain that the system is duplicating defects, but it will actually be two objects with different unique IDs. Most people understand this issue and can avoid the pitfall.

Something less intuitive is creating an object that most users don't use, using the unique ID (e.g., the release or the product name) as the primary way to refer to the object. If you have releases and products as objects in your system, and each unique ID is not the name commonly used by the users when referring to them, it can become very confusing.

Hopefully you're starting to see a theme here: Most development organizations are very temperamental when it comes to their tools. They want them to work correctly the first time out, so understanding each of these issues and planning accordingly is critical.

When you detect a situation like this, it's best to fix it as soon as possible. The easiest way to solve this problem is to rename one of the records or just remove one of the records (make sure it's not the one your engineer just updated!). If there is information in one of the records that you wish to keep, you will need to merge the information from one record to the other.

This is a manual process, as ClearQuest doesn't have a merge tool for records. However, there are a variety of tools for changing the different types of objects in the database. These object types are described in the following subsections.

Workspace Objects

To change workspace objects, just rename one of the objects so that both show up in the ClearQuest Client and ClearQuest Web applications. You must go to the site that has mastership of the object, then right-click on the object and select Rename from the context menu. Make sure that you don't name it something that already exists, or you'll just create another naming conflict.

Stateless Records

First, find the record that has a naming conflict. The easiest way to find these records is to query and filter using the ratl_keysite field. If you have two records with the same name and different ratl_keysite values, then you have a naming conflict. Second, make sure that you are at the site that has mastership of the record, and rename the record. Of course, also make sure that you don't create another conflict.

User Objects

[S.12.5] User objects need to be resolved in a very similar way, but there are some small differences. First, if you log in as an ambiguous user, you will receive the following error: `"User name 'xxx' is ambiguous; rename or qualify with '<'SITE'>' to proceed."` To change the name of the user, you must use the ClearQuest Designer tool. Go to the menu item Tools → User Administration to open the User Administration window (Figure 12–3). Double-click on the user name you want to modify.

Now, edit the user name by right-clicking on it and then selecting Edit User. You should see the dialog box shown in Figure 12–4.

Change the user name, and then click OK.

Next, you need to update the database by selecting DB Action → Upgrade (Figure 12–5).

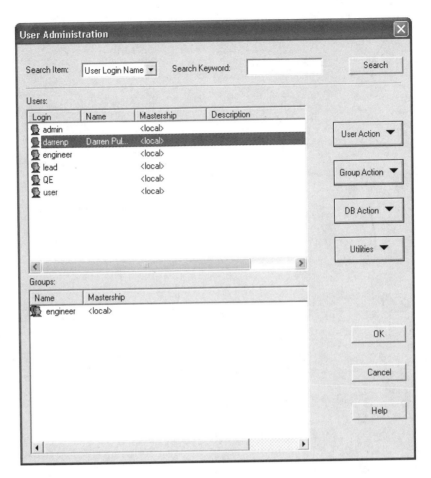

Figure 12–3 *Selecting a user*

Once you have finished, you will need to synchronize the sites for all of the changes to take effect.

ClearQuest MultiSite Design

Now that you understand the basics of ClearQuest MultiSite, it's time to make some decisions. You need to design your multisite deployment. A multisite deployment affects not only sites, families, and

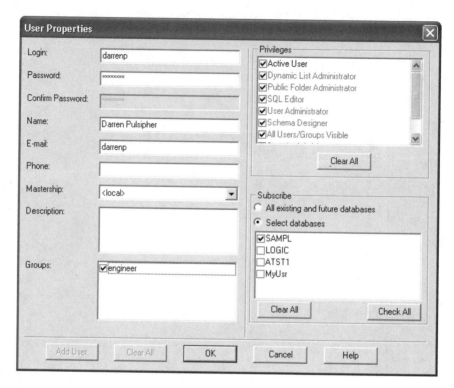

Figure 12–4   *Editing user information*

clans, but also the way people work together. Having a well-planned design is important. The key aspects to think about are described in the following subsections.

Mastership

The key to designing mastership is to make it as automated as possible. The fewer times a human needs to change mastership, the fewer

Figure 12–5   *Updating the database*

times mistakes and bottlenecks in the workflow will occur. So, automating the mastership is the best way to go. Even better is to avoid mastership changes, if at all possible. We can't stress this point enough: The fewer times you need to change mastership, the better off you will be.

Remember that all operations on an object are happening at the site, as in these examples.

- [S.12.6] Hooks that modify records or field values can run only if the current replica masters the record.

- You must modify users and groups at the replica that masters the user or group.

- You must edit workspace items (queries, reports, and report formats) at the master replica.

- You can modify or customize schemas only at the working schema repository.

Typically, automated mastership changes happen with record objects and are tied to the workflow that you have designed. If you have to change mastership, here are two areas to consider where they can happen automatically.

1. [S.12.7] *Action hooks*: Look at your workflow and determine where the mastership should be, depending on the state of an object and the action that needs to be performed. It's best to move the mastership *before* someone at another site needs the object. Don't change mastership on demand; it can be slow, and the user may rebel against the tool. Rely on your synchronization timing to sync the mastership changes.

2. *Periodic updates*: You can do this by using a scheduled mastership change that looks through the records at a site, changes the mastership of records as needed (based on record type, state, and field values), and then calls `syncreplica -export`. This method is actually very useful because you know when

things will be sent over. It also gives a grace period for a record if the current mastership site needs to make additional—and unexpected—changes. The downside is that mastership can be changed out from underneath someone using the object.

Synchronization

A synchronization strategy determines how often the sites will be synced and how they will be synced together. There are several different strategies for syncing sites. The main questions to ask yourself about sync strategies are as follows.

1. What families need to be synced?

2. How often do they need to be synced?

3. Where is the primary mastership site?

4. How many sites does the mastership site need to be synced to?

5. How is the information going to be transported?

6. What about disaster recovery and backups?

The first question is the most important. If you implement a sync strategy and find out later that your organization can actually get along without syncing any families, you just wasted time and money, so start by deciding what really needs to be synced. Remember that a family is basically all of the replicas at all of the sites for a particular database. It's good to understand the type of database, the uses of the database, and the users of the database family. This information will help answer the other questions.

The answer to the second question should be determined by how up-to-date you need your sites to be and how much potential data will be moving back and forth among the different sites for the family. If your sites are 3,000 miles and eight time zones from each other, then syncing every 15 minutes is probably not warranted. However, if they're one time zone away, and there is significant overlap in working hours, then syncing every 15 minutes may be valid. Additionally, if you are sending really large packets of information, then the export-transport-import mechanism may take longer than the sync interval. Therefore, you may want to decrease the sync time to decrease the amount of data for each sync operation.

How you answer the third question can play an important role in how often the family needs to be synced. You should consider mastership in your sync design. The answer will also help determine the sync configuration for your family.

[S.12.8] The fourth question may seem kind of funny, but you may not want all of your databases synced to all of your sites. Why not? It could be disk space constraints, security issues, or network transport bandwidth. It could be a number of reasons. The first thought in most of our minds is to sync everywhere, but you may want to take some time on this question. Only sync to the locations that you know need the information. Things can be added later if needed, but it is harder to take things away.

The fifth question is also not so obvious. Your first thought is most likely over the Internet or through your intranet. However, that's not sufficient. Are you going to use the ClearQuest shipping server, FTP, HTTP, or some secure network protocol? Consider that it may be faster to use what some call the FedEx network. Shipping a tape or CD in the mail may be more secure, faster, and more reliable. You never know. Find out the best mechanism for your organization, and include the details in your plan.

The final question is all about how you are going to back up your databases. Disaster recovery is a critical issue. If you have your backups in the same location as your master databases, that's a mistake. You need to have some location that is not physically close to the other sites that is dedicated to performing backups. This gives you the ability to recover in case of natural or manmade disasters.

Once you have answered all of these questions, you can begin to look at the various synchronization strategies. There are several different configurations to sync between sites. The key is to use the best combination for your environment. The answers to the questions should help you choose one of the configurations described in the following subsections.

One-to-One Synchronization

This method is used to sync two sites, and only two sites (Figure 12–6).

Most other configurations have some type of one-to-one synchronization.

Ring Synchronization

Ring synchronization consists of, well, syncs in a ring. Not all of the sites talk to teach other—they talk only to their neighbors (Figure 12–7).

This configuration is good for small multisite configurations.

Single-Hub Synchronization

When the number of sites in a configuration increases, you will probably want to move to a hub configuration (Figure 12–8).

This will limit the number of connections and time spent syncing sites. The bonus to this method is less time for syncups than a ring configuration. However, if the hub goes down, all sites are no longer being synced.

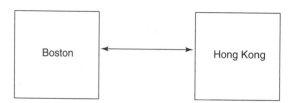

Figure 12–6   *One-to-one synchronization*

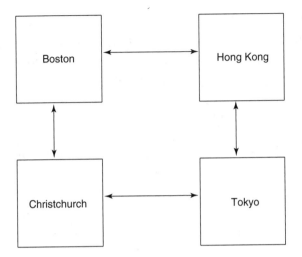

Figure 12–7   *Ring synchronization*

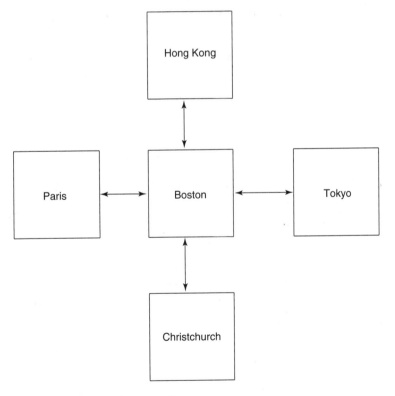

Figure 12–8   *Single-hub synchronization*

Multiple-Hub Synchronization

As the number of sites increases, you will need to add more sites to your central hub. This will slow down the hub dramatically and might make your syncups take longer than the prescribed sync interval. Another option is to add another hub and perform a one-to-one sync between the hubs (Figure 12–9).

Again, if one of the hubs goes down, then all spokes to the hub will not be synced.

Tree Synchronization

The tree sync is primarily used for syncs that must be very fast. It takes the hub idea and expands it further (Figure 12–10).

The downside to using a tree sync is that if one of the sites is down, it will affect all of the sites underneath.

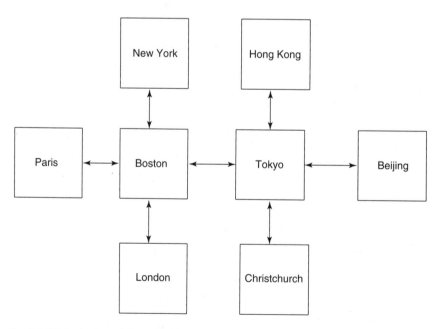

Figure 12–9 *Multiple-hub synchronization*

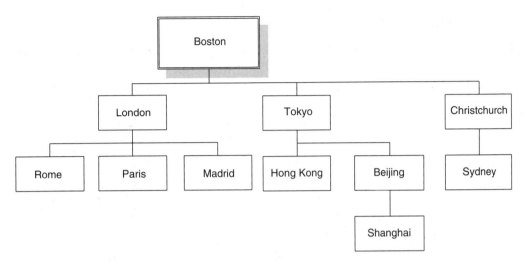

Figure 12–10 *Tree synchronization*

Many-to-Many Synchronization

This is the most redundant way to keep all of the sites synced together (Figure 12–11). The downside to this method is that it can take a long time to do all of the syncups.

If you have a lot of data, you should avoid this method.

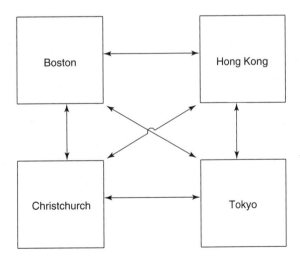

Figure 12–11 *Many-to-many synchronization*

Workflow

Once you have your sync configuration and your mastership scheme selected, it's time to start looking at your workflow to understand what changes, if any, will occur in the way your team works.

Specifically, you should look at where things are created in your model, where the various objects are owned, and how mastership and ownership of the different records change during the workflow. Take the following example: If you have a development team that is spread across Paris and Boston, where the team in Paris is primarily customer-facing and a testing organization, and the Boston team basically fixes the problems that the Paris team finds, then you may have a state net for a defect record that looks something like Figure 12–12.

Notice that the mastership changes between Paris and Boston. When the Boston team is done working on the defect, the mastership goes back to Paris.

This sort of workflow design needs to happen for all of the records in your system that will span more than one site. If a site just needs to look at a record and will not change any field or the state of the record, then mastership does not need to be changed.

Administration

Another aspect of multisite design is administration. You need to make sure you design the ability to handle multisite administration into your schema. Some people may provide the administrator with a table that contains valuable information such as the last sync of a family, the size and amount of time that it took to sync, and so forth. Here's a hint: Check the ClearQuest MultiSite manual for the types of records that are already created for a multisite replica, and add additional fields as necessary.

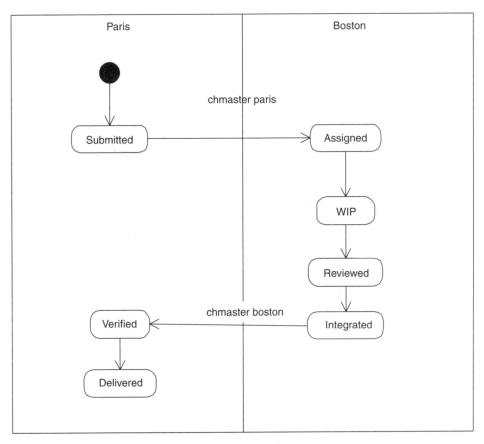

Figure 12–12   *Example of a state net diagram*

ClearQuest MultiSite and Tool Integration

[S.12.9] Using only ClearQuest in multisite mode within a system that has other integrated tools is a mistake. You need to configure *all* tools within the integration to work in multisite mode. If multisite capabilities are not available, then you should make sure that the integration is loosely coupled with these tools to avoid causing problems at other sites.

Just as with your ClearQuest MultiSite design, you need to determine when, what, how often, where, and how multisite usage of these other tools will happen. It's best to try to sync the ClearQuest data and the other tool data at the same time, if possible.

An example of synchronizing tools that are integrated is ClearQuest and ClearCase. In the example case we've been using, you could easily sync the ClearQuest family for DEV and the source VOBs for development at the same time. By using this method, changes that are made to the states of records for a defect or change request can have the source code synced at the same time.

You need to be mindful of errors here. In fact, we suggest having some centralized reporting structure to handle reporting errors in any of the systems, to alert you immediately when something fails. One thing to watch for is when one of the tools syncs successfully while another tool fails its synchronization (Figure 12–13); this leads to both tools being out of sync, as one is out of sync with the other locations while the other is out of sync with its integrated tool.

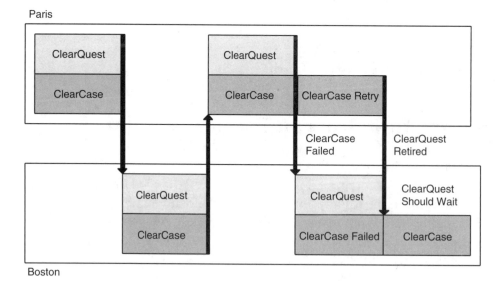

Figure 12–13   *Sites out of sync*

In this example, a sync of ClearCase fails in the second export from Paris. The ClearQuest sync should not fire again until the ClearCase sync is successful. If the ClearQuest sync is allowed to happen, then the Boston site's ClearQuest instance will be out of sync with its ClearCase instance.

What's needed is a mechanism to delay the ClearQuest sync until the ClearCase sync is successful. This policy is not the only way to handle situations like this, of course. You could always just go on syncing and not enforce tight synchronization between tools, but this can be very dangerous if your integration is bidirectional. In other words, if your systems need to share data back and forth, any sync issues will challenge the integrity of the overall system.

The key here is to come up with a policy and stick with it. Remember the problems that could occur should you just ignore the synchronization between tools and their integrations. Plan accordingly.

ClearQuest MultiSite Implementation

Before starting your multisite implementation, you should back up everything. Save this copy in several easily accessible locations and also in hard copy (CD or tape). It's unlikely that you'll get everything right the first time; having a backup copy is always a good idea.

Once you have a backup, the first thing you should do is work on your documentation. You need to make sure you have the following documented:

- The workflow for using multiple sites, including mastership of objects
- The sites and the sync configuration you have chosen for your system
- The frequency with which families will be synced

- The method of transporting the sync packets

- The multisite integration strategy

Once you have documented these things, you're ready to start implementing the design. For best results, you should adhere to the following steps to create your replicas and start multisite syncups.

1. *Store-and-forward configuration*: If you will use store-and-forward, you must configure the shipping.conf file (UNIX) or MultiSite Control Panel (Windows) at the exporting and importing replicas. Look at the MultiSite installation manual for more information about the shipping.conf file.

2. *Export*: Enter an `mkreplica -export` command, which creates a new replica object and a replica creation packet.

3. *Transport*: Send the replica creation packet to one or more other sites.

4. *Database creation*: At the location where the new replica is to be created, create empty vendor databases for the schema repository and each user database replica.

5. [S.12.10] *Import*: At the location where the new replica is to be created, import the replica creation packet by using `mkreplica -import`.

Database Set Activation

If you have not already activated the database set, then you will need to do so at this time. Remember that the database set includes the schema repository and all of the user databases.

To activate the database set, use the `activate` command. (See the ClearQuest Command manual for more information about this command.)

Export

ClearQuest has tools that allow for the export of information necessary for creating a replica for a remote site. The command to use to create the replica is `mkreplica -export`.

Before using this command to make a replica, do the following.

- Make sure that all of the users are logged out of the database.
- Make sure that all of the user databases are updated to the latest version of the schema.
- Make sure that the data code pages are the same at all sites.

In the following example, a replica of the DEV user database and its schema repository is created from the Boston site. The target site is named `paris`; it uses the machine `triumph`. This example uses store-and-forward to ship the replica creation packets. The clan of the multisite is named `bloqs`.

```
multiutil mkreplica -export -clan bloqs -site boston
  -family DEV
-user dallin -password passwd -maxsize 50m -fship
-workdir c:\temp\packets -sclass cq_default triumph:paris
```

For more information on creating replicas, see the ClearQuest Command manual for several examples on creating mechanisms.

Database Creation

Before calling the import of the packets that have been transported from the creation site to the target site, you must create the vendor database for the information to be imported. Do not create the databases with ClearQuest Designer. If you do this, the import will fail. Creating the databases with ClearQuest Designer or the Administration tool will cause an import failure. You are only required to create the vendor databases. See the ClearQuest Administration manual for the creation of vendor databases.

Import

Now that you have created the vendor databases and the packets have been transported to the remote target location, you need to log into the remote location and call `mkreplica -import`. The following example shows how to import the packets that were created earlier.

```
multiutil mkreplica -import -site paris -repository paris
  _schemarepo
-vendor SQL_SERVER -server triumph -dbologin dallin passwd
-rwlogin dallin passwd -rologin dallin passwd -database
  paris_dev
-vendor SQL_SERVER -dbologin dallin passwd -rwlogin dallin
  passwd
```

The packets will be imported into the SQL_server database on the machine `triumph`. Two databases, `paris_schemarepo` and `paris_dev`, will be used to import the data contained in the packets. For more information about importing replicas, look at the Clear-Quest Command manual.

Syncups

[S.12.11] Once the replicas for the families have been created and things are set up, you need to set up the synchronization rules and set the times at which the locations need to sync. Remember, the basic flow of syncing replicas in a family is as follows:

- *Export*: Use `syncreplica -export` at the local site.
- *Transport*: Packets are sent to one or more sites.
- *Import*: Use `syncreplica -import` at the remote site.

Use this basic mechanism to implement the synchronization configuration you have designed. You need to either set up a crontab or use the Rational Scheduler to set up how often the sites will be synced.

Adding some kind of reporting system to your syncing mechanism can make things easier to see and monitor over time. You'll be able to find errors that occur in any one of the steps. For more information on these individual steps, see the ClearQuest Command manual for information on `syncreplica`.

Oplogs and Epoch Numbers

ClearQuest keeps track of the changes made to each replica through a mechanism called *epoch numbers*. To minimize the data that needs to be transported, ClearQuest sends only the changes that have been made to each replica. This information is kept in *oplogs* (operation logs). The oplogs contain the number of changes as counted by epoch numbers.

ClearQuest keeps track of the following epoch numbers.

- *Changes made in the current replica*: This one is obvious: All changes to the current replica need to be accounted for. This is used when ClearQuest is determining what needs to be shipped to the sibling replicas.

- *Changes to sibling replicas that have been imported into the current replica*: This epoch number is important in determining how much has already been synced to the current replica. This gives ClearQuest the information it needs to make sure that duplicate operations from the oplogs have not been replicated to the current replica. It is also used to make sure that all of the entries in the oplogs have been processed.

- *Estimates of the states of other replicas*: This epoch number corresponds to the number exported to remote sibling replicas. It makes the assumption that the sibling replica has imported all operations in the oplog successfully. This prevents ClearQuest from sending more information than it needs to send to keep things in sync.

Epoch tables and oplogs can get confusing very quickly. The key is to remember where you are—in other words, what machine, what location, and what replica you're working with—when you look at the epoch table.

In the following example, we have two replicas, lehi_site and tokyo_site.

- Each time work occurs in the lehi_site replica, ClearQuest increments its associated epoch number.

- When the lehi_site replica imports updates from tokyo_site, ClearQuest updates its associated row and the row associated with tokyo_site in the epoch table.

- When the lehi_site replica exports changes to be sent to tokyo_site, ClearQuest changes the tokyo_site row in the epoch table.

The best way to see this is to look at an example of an epoch table (Table 12–2) and see what happens in each case. Remember that each replica records the number of changes it has made to itself, the changes it has received from another replica, and the changes it has sent to another replica. (This example is on the machine that hosts the lehi_site replica.)

Note that the values in the table are obtained from running the lsepoch command on the machine that hosts the lehi_site replica:

Table 12–2   *Epoch Table*

	Operations Originated at the Lehi Site	Operations Originated at the Tokyo Site
lehi_site's record of its own state	875	408
lehi_site's estimate of tokyo_site's state	862	408

```
Multiutil lsepoch -clan xango -site lehi_site -family FNDRY
-user admin -password foobar

Multiutil: Estimates of the epochs from each site
replayed at site 'lehi_site' (@mangosteen):
lehi_site: 875
tokyo_site: 408
Multiutil: Estimates of the epochs from each site
replayed at site 'tokyo_site' (@samida):
lehi_site: 862
tokyo_site: 408
```

This basically says that lehi_site is out of sync with tokyo_site. Why? Because tokyo_site has an epoch number of 862 for lehi_site, while the lehi_site epoch number is really at 875. This means that when syncreplica -export is run from lehi_site, ClearQuest will put together a packet(s) containing the changes from 862 to 875.

Once the syncreplica -export command has been called, ClearQuest will update the epoch table for the lehi_site replica as follows:

```
Multiutil lsepoch -clan xango -site lehi_site -family FNDRY
-user admin -password foobar

Multiutil: Estimates of the epochs from each site replayed
  at site 'lehi_site' (@mangosteen):
lehi_site: 875
tokyo_site: 408
Multiutil: Estimates of the epochs from each site replayed
  at site 'tokyo_site' (@samida):
lehi_site: 875
tokyo_site: 408
```

Note that the tokyo_site row with the lehi_site entry now has 875, stating that both replicas are in sync. However, this offers a false sense of success. This is what the lehi_site replica thinks, but it's not necessarily what the tokyo_site has received. The epoch has actually been updated only on the lehi_site replica so far, because the tokyo_site replica has not received the packet yet and the import has not been done. So if you go to the machine that hosts the tokyo_site replica, it will show that the changes have not been made yet.

Before the `tokyo_site` epoch numbers are updated in the `tokyo_site` replica, the packet from the `lehi_site` replica must be imported using the `Multiutil-import` command. If the import is successful, then it will update the number.

You're probably thinking, "Why in the world would ClearQuest do this? Epoch numbers here and there, what machine am I on? I'm getting ready to pull my hair out!" The epoch numbers on the import side of the transaction serve as a check to ensure that all operations are coming into the receiving replica in the correct order and not more than once. The `tokyo_site` replica will log an error if the packet it receives does not start with the epoch number it is expecting. It will then set the epoch number to the last epoch number in the import. This mechanism protects against data corruption between replicas.

When your users complain that they cannot see a change made at one location on all of the other locations, the `Multiutil -lsepoch` command is the right place to start. It will not tell you what's wrong, but it *can* tell you the state that things are in. Most of the time, replicas get out of sync due to the transport of the packets from one site to another. So, start looking at disk space or network connectivity if you see things out of sync.

Managing a Replica Syncup

With the `Multiutil -lsepoch` command, ClearQuest can give you an idea that things are out of sync. Also, plowing through logs can help you determine why syncs are not happening. The following are the typical reasons for replicas to get out of sync.

- ClearQuest cannot find the oplog entry.

- Packets accumulate in outgoing storage and incoming storage.

- Transportation configuration problems occur.

- A packet has an invalid destination.

- Delivery of a packet fails due to a network connectivity problem.

- There is not enough disk space to generate a packet on the export or import side.

- The shipping server goes down.

- The shipping order expires.

- Packets are processed slowly on the import or export side.

- Solar flares on the sun knock out satellite communication between sites.

The following subsections explore your options for recovering from syncup problems.

Recovering Packets

Now that you know you have a problem, what do you do? This is why you get paid the big bucks: You have to figure out what's not in sync and then fix it. We suggest the following steps.

- Tell your boss that it is a very complex and convoluted process and that only experts like you can fix it.

- Find out where things are not in sync. Run the `Multiutil` `-lsepoch` command on each of the machines of the replicas and find out which one is out of sync.

- Run the `Multiutil recoverpacket` command on the machine that is sending packets to the sibling replica. This command resets the estimates for a remote replica within the current replica's epoch table. It can be set to a date/time or to the current value on the remote replica. In the following example, ClearQuest resets the epoch number back to the value as of April 17, 2005:

```
Multiutil recoverpacket -clan xango -site lehi_site
   -family
FNDRY -user admin -password foobar -since 17-April-2005
   tokyo_site
```

```
Multiutil: Using epoch information from 17-Apr-2005
  .00:00:00.
Multiutil: Epoch estimates for replica 'tokyo_site'
  successfully reset.

TOKYO_SITE: 430
```

Now the `lehi_site` epoch table has an entry for `tokyo_site` at 430. So, the next time `export` is run, it will generate a packet for all oplogs entries starting at 430 until the present.

Recovering Replicas

If you're reading this section, either you have a general interest in the tool or you are neck deep in a disaster and you need to get your replicas back. If you start down this road, you have probably had a major catastrophe; we feel your pain. It's probably 2:30 A.M., so the parking lot should be deserted. (If not, use your own judgment with regard to what we say next.) The best thing to do right now is to set this book down and go out into the parking lot and scream at the top of your lungs. Get out all of that frustration. It doesn't matter at whom you are frustrated—the replicas need to be recovered.

Now that you have a clearer head, let's get down into what to do if you have a completely corrupt or lost replica.

First, check your backups. (If you don't have backups—in other words, if you haven't been following our advice, for some reason—you can back up from another replica. Just keep in mind that you will lose information from the replica you're trying to restore if it has not been backed up or synced with another replica. So, if you synced three hours ago, you will have lost "only" three hours' worth of work.)

Now that you have selected your replica or backup, it's time to clean up the mess that is before you.

- First, restore the database backup with your database restore utility. This varies with the database vendor that you're using.

- Use the `restorereplica` command to start the restoration procedure.

- Verify that all update packets have been processed at their destination replicas.

- Generate update packets for all other replicas in the family using the `syncreplica -export` command.

- Make sure that each replica in the family has sent an update packet to the restored replica.

- Process all incoming packets with the command `syncreplica -import`.

The ClearQuest Command manual pages offer more detailed information, under `restorereplica`.

If you have kept your replicas updated frequently, another option is to destroy the bad replica and create a new one. The only downside to this is that if you have a very large database, it could take a while to create the new replica. The next subsection describes how to remove a broken replica. Once you have done that, you can create a new replica as described earlier in this chapter.

Removing a Broken Replica

Sometimes a database is broken beyond repair and needs to be removed. It can be recreated at a later time or just removed for good.

In the following example, the `sojo_site` replica will be removed from the FNDRY family. `tokyo_site` and `lehi_site` are part of the same clan as the `sojo_site` replica.

1. Change the mastership of all objects from the broken replica to another replica.

   At `lehi_site` (schema repository site), run this command:

```
Multiutil chmaster -clan xango -site lehi_site -family
FNDRY -user admin -password foobar lehi_site -all -force
sojo_site
```

Note that the -family is FNDRY.

The next step changes the mastership on MASTR.

2. Force transfer of mastership for all users and groups.

At lehi_site (schema repository site), run this command:

```
Multiutil chmaster -clan xango -site lehi_site -family
MASTR -user admin -password foobar lehi_site -all -force
sojo_site
```

3. At the working schema site, run rmreplica to remove the broken replica.

4. At lehi_site (schema repository site), run this command:

```
Multiutil rmreplica -clan xango -site lehi_site -family
FNDRY -user admin -password foobar sojo_site
```

Make sure that the last argument is the replica that you are removing.

5. Remove the schema repository with the rmreplica command.

6. At lehi_site (schema repository site), run this command:

```
Multiutil rmreplica -clan xango -site lehi_site -family
MASTR -user admin -password foobar sojo_site
```

Make sure that the last argument is the replica that you are removing.

7. Send an update packet from the working schema repository site to all of the sites.

8. At lehi_site (schema repository site), run this command:

```
Multiutil syncreplica -export -clan xango -site lehi_site
  -family
FNDRY -user admin -password foobar -fship tokyo_site
```

9. At `tokyo_site`, run this command:

```
Multiutil syncreplica -import -clan xango -site tokyo_site
-family FNDRY -user admin -password foobar -receive
```

10. Remove the vendor database from the replica and schema repository that you removed. Make sure you are on the machine for the site that is being removed. (It would *not* be good if you removed the schema repository site.)

Keeping a Multisite Deployment Organized

One of the most important things you can do to keep your ClearQuest MultiSite system maintained involves documenting what you have done. Every time you create a new site, make sure to update your design document. Make sure that your documentation reflects the architecture you originally put together. There's nothing more frustrating than trying to find out what's happening with a dynamic system when you have not documented the static (stable) system.

Another great tool that most people overlook is a maintenance log. Buy a bound notebook (the kind they made you have in school). Page numbers are good but not necessary. Make sure that any maintenance or changes you make to the system are logged in this book. The best place to keep it is where your team can access it. Although archaic, this tool is invaluable when trying to figure out what has happened.

Note: Do *not* keep this maintenance log online. As you know, machines have a tendency to go down, and data gets lost.

Finally, have an outlet for frustration and get a sense of humor. Dealing with multisite systems is not a trivial task, and you are typically dealing with multiple time zones and communication problems that range from language idioms and accents to static on the line. On those long, lonely nights in the computer lab, just remember that there are hundreds if not thousands of others, just like you, trying to get things ready for the software development masses first thing in the morning.

developerWorks Links

A.12.1   http://www-128.ibm.com/developerworks/rational/ library/4678.html

S.12.1   http://www-128.ibm.com/developerworks/rational/ library/4518.html

S.12.2   http://www-128.ibm.com/developerworks/rational/ library/3929.html

A.12.2   http://www-128.ibm.com/developerworks/rational/ library/6000.html

S.12.3   http://www-128.ibm.com/developerworks/rational/ library/4354.html

S.12.4   http://www-128.ibm.com/developerworks/rational/ library/05/412_howell/

T.12.1   http://www-128.ibm.com/developerworks/edu/i-dw -r-rmultisite-i.html

S.12.5   http://www-128.ibm.com/developerworks/rational/ library/3918.html

S.12.6   http://www-128.ibm.com/developerworks/rational/library/4383.html

S.12.7   http://www-128.ibm.com/developerworks/rational/library/4354.html

S.12.8   http://www-128.ibm.com/developerworks/rational/library/4514.html

S.12.9   http://www-128.ibm.com/developerworks/rational/library/4385.html

S.12.10   http://www-128.ibm.com/developerworks/rational/library/4332.html

S.12.11   http://www-128.ibm.com/developerworks/rational/library/4391.html

Epilogue

One of the most common complaints about most applications—and ClearQuest is no exception—is that the standard documentation does not provide adequate guidance and best practices for deployment. Even when you find deployment and integration guidelines, they often lack some of the business reasoning behind them to help you reinforce the importance of the new or expanded application to your management team. And, in most cases, they fail to take into account how the new application fits into, or affects, the other tools in the change management continuum.

With flexibility comes complexity, and what is needed is a plan for continuous fine-tuning. Your systems will change, your back-end requirements may shift depending on your partners and vendors, but your change control systems should be able to manage these changes.

Your change management system is the glue that binds your engineering, testing, manufacturing, and product development organizations, intrinsically tying them to your customers. This is the medium through which process is enforced and communication tracked. Part of your planning should establish a continual change management process and tool assessment to ensure that your users' needs are being met and that the system is updated as new products and add-ons are released. We know it sounds like a no-brainer, but if you don't plan for system optimization, it usually doesn't happen—until something breaks.

The Change Agent

The primary value of an application such as ClearQuest is to improve communication across the organization—between product and development teams, between production and support, and between company and customer. No more endless volleying between product management and engineering and engagement personnel to clarify exactly what the customer wants and needs and what the development team can deliver; in combination with ClearCase and other tools in the IBM Rational Suite, ClearQuest is the communication vehicle for your change management system.

And you are the change agent making it all possible—whether you're the company's official change management manager or just a part of the change management team trying to understand how ClearQuest fits into the picture. Integration of ClearQuest into your company's hodgepodge of different development, test, change management, and project management tools doesn't just happen on its own. It requires formal analysis, design, and implementation cycles to identify and validate the benefits, and several change agents from throughout the organization to ensure that it's done properly and with input from all the potential user organizations. Far too many change management systems are grown organically over time; the result is fragile, rigid systems in constant need of upgrades and repair. While these systems create job security for some engineers, they often become management nightmares.

Now that you have a better understanding of where ClearQuest fits into the change management continuum and how to deploy it properly, the key is to plan your implementation thoroughly. As you undertake this project, make sure you have the proper support from management and input from the relevant teams to accomplish your task. Change management systems are probably among the more difficult solutions to develop and deploy. You are tasked with integrating several systems that need to act as one system. Your solution must be highly reliable, and your deployment cannot affect the current development cycle. So make sure you do your homework.

Shameless Plug

[A.13.1] If you're also looking to roll out IBM Rational's ClearCase as part of your software configuration management solution, we recommend that you look at our book *The Art of ClearCase® Deployment* (Addison-Wesley, 2004). As with this book, we cover the entire solution space around the application, not just the technical aspects.

Our other book follows some of the same technical footsteps you'll find in your product documentation, but as with this book, it provides the material in a way that a broader group of project personnel can use. Our goal with both of these books was to provide members of the extended project team—and burgeoning change management managers—with a better understanding of how an end-to-end change management solution, in general, can enhance an organization's ability to deliver better products, faster.

Additional Resources

Whether you have questions about specific functionality or you want to prepare yourself for some custom work on your ClearQuest install, your options online are constantly growing. IBM Rational provides a wealth of content through the developerWorks site. A number of vendors and partners also offer specific answers.

While not every site we include here has the stamp of approval from IBM Rational, it's always good to see what other project teams are doing and what the various add-on vendors are selling. Here are some recommended websites at which you might begin your research.

- http://www-136.ibm.com/developerworks/rational/
  This is the main IBM Rational website, providing links to online technical documentation, downloads, online seminars, and many other valuable tools and links.

- http://www.cmcrossroads.com
  CM Crossroads is *the* configuration management community online, with articles, product reviews and comparisons, web casts, and discussion forums. If you want to share your experiences with the community at large or want to find out about other efforts to integrate ClearQuest with a variety of applications, this is the place to start your research.

- http://www.rational-ug.org/
  The Rational Software Global User Group Community website provides access to independent, user-run groups around the world where you can exchange information with other users and IBM Rational staff in live or virtual meetings.

- http://www-136.ibm.com/developerworks/rational/community
  Of course, the IBM Rational website provides links to relevant content and groups for each of its products.

- http://www-306.ibm.com/software/support/assistance.html
  This is the IBM Rational Help page. It provides an overview of
  the various support documents available on the website and
  within the technical support knowledge base. It also includes
  site tours, helping you to better learn how to navigate the ex-
  pansive website.

- http://www-306.ibm.com/software/support/help.html
  Finally, if you discover you have a technical problem that cannot be resolved without IBM Rational's help (or heavenly in-
  tervention), you'll need to become acquainted with IBM's
  Electronic Service Request (ESR) problem submission tool.
  The ESR helps you through the process of reporting issues,
  ensuring that all of the proper fields and descriptions during
  the creation or update of your Problem Management Records
  (PMRs) are filled out to the best of your ability.

developerWorks Links

A.13.1   http://www-128.ibm.com/developerworks/rational/
library/469.html

Index

Documentation (product). *See* Publications.
Documentation (user environment)
   team advocate, 8–9
   value of, 5
Dropdown Combo Box controls, 132
Dropdown combo boxes, 132
Dropdown List Box controls, 132
Dropdown list boxes, 132
Dual-system migration, 236–237
Duplicate action, 124
Duplicate Box controls, 132
Duplicate records
   creating, 124
   displaying ID of, 132
Dynamic choice lists, 115, 116–118
DYNAMIC option, 115

E

Eclipse
   client pros and cons, 140–141
   overview, 139–140
   perspectives, 149, 150–151
   plug-in
     configuring, 141–148
     customizing, 148–149
     database connections, 142–144
     downloading, 141
     e-mail options, 144–145
     installing, 141–148
     logging in to databases, 142
     MultiSite support, 146–148
     preferences, 148–149
     remembering passwords, 142
     user profiles, 145–146
     versus Windows client, 162–163
   queries. *See also* Queries.
     creating, 157–163
     deleting, 165
     editing, 163–164
     executing, 167–170
     filters, 158–160
     renaming, 165
     saving, 164–165
     SQL version, viewing, 166
     viewing results, 167–169, 170–171
   Eclipse, records. *See also* Records.
     attachments
       creating, 179
       deleting, 179–180
       opening, 180
     creating, 176–177

     finding, 178
     performing actions on, 172–176
     refreshing, 176
     viewing information, 171–172
     viewing record information, 171–172
Eclipse, views
   Console, 153
   definition, 149
   Navigator, 151–153
   Query Results
     overview, 153–154
     performing actions on records, 172–176
     refreshing records, 176
     viewing query results, 169–172
   Record Details
     overview, 153–154
     performing actions on records, 175–176
     viewing record information, 171–172
   Tasks, 155–156
Eclipse records
   performing actions on, 172–176
   viewing information, 171–172
   viewing record information, 171–172
Edison, Thomas, 183
Edit Query Wizard, 163–164. *See also* Query Wizard.
Editing queries, 163–164
E-mail
   automatic change request notification, 56
   Eclipse plug-in options, 144–145
   integrating tools, 37
   integration with ClearQuest, 185
   Rational E-Mail Reader, 50
Email package, 191
E-Mail Reader, 50
End state, 79–80
Engineers, buy-in, 19–20
Enhancement Request package, 192
Enhancement requests, 8–9
Enterprise schema, 61
Enterprise schemas, 61
EnterpriseStudio, 61, 87
Epoch numbers, 265–268
Exceptional flow of events, 67–68
Executing queries, 167–170
Executive team, buy-in, 21
Export Tool, 50
Exporting data
   from databases, 50
   MultiSite, 263
   for replicas, 263
Extended configuration, 228

Repository corruption, 12
Repository maintenance. *See* Maintenance Tool.
Repository package, 193
Requirements analysis. *See* Needs analysis.
Requirements management, 36–37
RequisitePro, 61, 87, 185
RequisitePro actors, 66
RequisitePro package, 194
Resolution package, 194
Restricting access. *See* Access restrictions.
Reviewing change requests, 55
Ring synchronization, 254–255
Roadmap to ClearQuest success, 8–10
Rules, 61
Rumbaugh, James, 76
RUP (Rational Unified Process). *See* Rational Unified Process (RUP).

S
Saving queries, 164–165
Scenarios. *See also* Activity diagrams; Use cases; User interface design.
  examples, 23–25
  importance of, 23
  in use cases, 68–70
Schema repositories
  creating, 221–223
  definition, 59, 220
  maintenance. *See* Maintenance Tool.
  types, 242–243
Schemas
  adding packages to, 186–188
  adding UCM, 202–212
  AnalystStudio, 61, 87
  Blank, 61, 87
  Common, 61, 87
  contents, 58
  creating, 94–98
  customizing, 58–62, 105–106
  database associations, 59, 94–98
  DefectTracking, 61, 87
  definition, 58
  DevelopmentStudio, 61, 87
  Enterprise, 61, 87
  existing, 93–94
  managing. *See* ClearQuest Designer.
  naming, 94–95
  opening, 94
  predefined, 58–59, 61, 87
  scripting, 105–106

  selecting, 61–62
  testing, 61
  TestStudio, 61, 87
  UnifiedChangeManagement, 61, 87
Scott, Kendall, 76
Script Editor, 61
Scripts
  action hooks, 134
  associating scripts with records, 124
  BASIC, 105–106, 116
  choice lists, 116, 136
  and choice lists, 116
  field hooks, 134
  generating choice lists, 115–116
  hooks, 134
  languages, 105–106
  Perl, 105–106, 116
  UCM policy, 207–208
  UCU_ChkBeforeDeliver, 208
  UCU_ChkBeforeWorkOn, 208
  UCU_CQActAfterDeliver, 208
  UCU_CQActBeforeChact, 208
SCRIPTS option, 115
Simple configuration, 227–228
Single-hub synchronization, 254–255
Sites, 241–242
Software Configuration . . . and IBM Rational ClearCase, 198
Software defects. *See* Defects.
Software development environment, 51
SQL Anywhere, 101–102
SQL Server, 100–101
Standard queries, 52–53
Start state, 79–80
State
  adding actions, 123
  adding to records, 59, 119
  adding transitions, 119–122
  and change requests, 56
  changing, 124
  definition (ClearQuest), 48
  end, 79–80
  of objects, 79–80
  start, 79–80
  statechart diagrams, 79–80
  types (UCM), 203–206, 208–210
State nets, 118
State notation (UML), 79
State Transition Matrix, 59, 119–122
State-based records
  definition, 49, 109
  duplicating, 124

THIS BOOK IS SAFARI ENABLED

INCLUDES FREE 45-DAY ACCESS TO THE ONLINE EDITION

The Safari® Enabled icon on the cover of your favorite technology book means the book is available through Safari Bookshelf. When you buy this book, you get free access to the online edition for 45 days.

Safari Bookshelf is an electronic reference library that lets you easily search thousands of technical books, find code samples, download chapters, and access technical information whenever and wherever you need it.

TO GAIN 45-DAY SAFARI ENABLED ACCESS TO THIS BOOK:

- Go to **http://www.awprofessional.com/safarienabled**

- Complete the brief registration form

- Enter the coupon code found in the front of this book on the "Copyright" page

If you have difficulty registering on Safari Bookshelf or accessing the online edition, please e-mail customer-service@safaribooksonline.com.

Addison
Wesley